Start Your
RETAIL
Career

Other Entrepreneur Pocket Guides Include:

- *Buy or Lease a Car without Getting Taken for a Ride*
- *Dirty Little Secrets: What the Credit Bureaus Won't Tell You*
- *Get That Raise!*
- *How to Sell Automotive Parts and Accessories on eBay*
- *How to Sell Clothing, Shoes, and Accessories on eBay*
- *How to Sell Collectibles on eBay*
- *How to Sell Computers and Accessories on eBay*
- *How to Sell Health and Beauty Products on eBay*
- *How to Sell Jewelry and Watches on eBay*
- *How to Sell Toys and Hobbies on eBay*
- *Mortgages and Refinancing: Get the Best Rates*
- *Mutual Funds: A Quick-Start Guide*
- *Start Your Health Care Career*
- *Start Your Real Estate Career*
- *Start Your Restaurant Career*
- *Why Rent? Own Your Dream Home!*

Entrepreneur
MAGAZINE'S
POCKET GUIDES

Start Your
RETAIL
Career

*Entrepreneur Press
and Stephanie O'Malley*

EP
Entrepreneur
Press

Jere L. Calmes, Publisher
Cover Design: Beth Hansen-Winter
Production and Composition: Alicen Armstrong Brown

This publication is designed to provide accurate and authoritative information in regard to the subject matter covered. It is sold with the understanding that the publisher is not engaged in rendering legal, accounting,
or other professional services. If legal advice or other expert assistance is
required, the services of a competent professional person should be sought.

Library of Congress Cataloging-in-Publication Data
    Start your retail career/by Entrepreneur Press and Stephanie M.
    O'Malley.
      p. cm.
    ISBN-13: 978-1-59918-164-6 (alk. paper)
    ISBN-10: 1-59918-164-9 (alk. paper)
      1. Retail trade—Management. 2. New business enterprises.
    I. Entrepreneur Press. II. O'Malley, Stephanie M.
    HF5429.S72 2008
    658.8'70023—dc22   2007026670

Printed in Canada
12 11 10 09 08   10 9 8 7 6 5 4 3 2 1

Contents

Chapter 2

Is Retail Right for You? 19

Chapter 3

Jobs in the Store 39

Chapter 4

Jobs Outside the Store 69

Chapter 5
The Working Environment 101

Acknowledgments

First and foremost, I would like to thank business guru and author George Colombo, who has been the best of friends, and who made this book possible. Thanks also to Entrepreneur Press for giving me this opportunity, and especially to Courtney Thurman for all her hard work and Jere Calmes.

I would like to thank the following individuals, who so generously gave of their time to arrange interviews or to talk about their love of retail. Your stories are the heart of this book:

Deb Comeau, Keepsake Quilting, The Lakes Region, New Hampshire
Lyle Davis, Pastures of Plenty, Longmont, Colorado
Judith Catherine Duthie, McNally Robinson Booksellers, Calgary, Alberta, Canada

Mindy Miles Greenberg, Visual Merchant, New York,
   New York

Laurel Humphrey, Dallas, Texas

Kathleen Johnson, The Comfortable Home, Kittredge,
   Colorado

Lily Kender, University of Florida, Gainesville, Florida

Micheal Klein, William Noble Rare Jewels, Dallas, Texas

Rene MacLeod, Barnie's Coffee and Tea, Winter Springs,
   Florida

Suzanne Meriden, The Container Store, Costa Mesa,
   California

Rob O'Brian, Keepsake Quilting, The Lakes Region,
   New Hampshire

Shelley Petrilli, What a Girl Wants, Evergreen, Colorado

Cecilia M. Schulz, Betsy A. Trobaugh, University of Florida,
   Gainesville, Florida

Courtney Shaver, The Container Store, Costa Mesa, California

Al Slavin, Wal-Mart, San Antonio, Texas

Ken Slavin, Ken Slavin Public Relations, San Antonio, Texas

Sue Stewart, Consumer Focus, Dallas, Texas

Stanley Surman, The Men's Wearhouse, Altamonte Springs,
   Florida

Allison Trembly, Whole Foods Market, Lakewood, Colorado

Bo Wells, HoundsTooth Bakery, Winter Park, Florida

And finally, thanks to Sparky and Mojo for keeping my lap warm while I wrote this book, and to my wonderful family for their patience and support.

■ ■ ■

Preface

Welcome to world of retail. I should say welcome to the other side of the world of retail, the side behind the mirrors, the fabulous displays, and even the computer screen, because of course, as a consumer, you have been a part of retail nearly every day of your life. And now you may be considering a career in retail.

I've got great news for you: Retail is hotter than ever, and there's always plenty of room for smart, innovative people. The retail industry offers a greater variety of opportunities for the ambitious and hardworking than almost any other industry. If you love meeting new people and helping them find products to meet their wants and needs, then retail could be the place for you. If you're the analytical type who can discover ways to bolster sagging sales, then retail could also be the place for you. In other words, there's room for just about anyone who is committed and dedicated, and for people with many different talents.

To get the most out of this book, it helps to know how it's set up. Each chapter starts with the story of a real person working in retail, who can describe the ups and downs of the industry better than any statistic or study. These stories and the quiz at the end of Chapter 2 will, more than anything else, help you to determine if retail is right for you.

We then explore the industry in Chapters 3 and 4 by looking at jobs within stores, and at headquarters. Chapter 5 describes what it's like to work in certain subsectors of retail, such as department stores, grocery stores, or automotive retailers.

These chapters are chock-full of great information—job descriptions, earnings, educational requirements, and even the outlook for the future. Chapters 7 and 8 give you the tools to target potential employers, get hired, and then zoom ahead in your career.

Maybe you've always dreamed of going into business for yourself. Take the quiz in Chapter 9 to see if you're suited for life as an entrepreneur. If so, there's more than one way to do it. Read the stories of three terrific individuals who've taken the plunge, yet chosen very different routes.

And finally, good luck!

All about
Retail

my parents sent me to take tests, and through the tests I found that I was interested in art, music, and retail. I thought about being a professional musician, but that didn't pan out.

"I started in retail in my early 20s when I got out of school. There was an ad in the paper for Robert Hall clothes, and it sounded very appealing to me. I went into New York, and I interviewed with the president. And I have to say, I was very impressed. They had a wonderful training program. They assigned me to a store for training, and the program was in two-week segments. But then I was interrupted by a two-year stint in the army."

After serving his country, Surman returned to retail and to the training program, where he worked as an assistant manager for an extremely tough store manager. "I just couldn't please him, no matter what I did." Rather than give up, Surman came up with a new game plan. "I got up at 4 A.M. and got everything done by the time he arrived at noon. He was very impressed. Of course he didn't know I had been there since 4 A.M. I had my own keys, and I worked in the Times Square store." Surman went on to become great friends with the manager.

Later Surman went to work for what is now known as the Hartmarx Corporation and then for a company called Roots. Roots carried clothing that was extremely high-end. Surman well remembers his interview with Perry Root. "I was wearing a yellow and blue plaid all-weather coat, and he invited me to come in, take off the coat, and sit down. Then he told me to burn the coat, because it was so ugly," Surman laughs. But he got the job, in spite of the coat.

"I got a marvelous ongoing education at that job. The store was beautiful, with a gorgeous front door and chandeliers. I learned about Irish linen and Oriental rugs. But I eventually reached a plateau, and moved on."

Eventually, because Surman's family had all moved to Florida, he and his wife decided to make the move from the Northeast and go into semiretirement. He took a job at the Men's Wearhouse in Altamonte Springs, Florida. "They kept asking me to go into management, and I've been working for them for over ten years."

One of the things that Surman likes so much about his current job is the corporate culture, which stresses the importance of customer service. "The Men's Wearhouse is not a clothing company, but a people company." Each year the founder, George Zimmer, awards a trip to Hawaii to the outstanding sales associate, tailor, and store manager in recognition of exceptional customer service.

Surman says he believes certain traits lead to success in retail. "When I am hiring, I look for enthusiasm. I'm amazed by the young people who come to work for us—they've got great work ethic."

"You have to apply yourself and do everything you can to make your mark. You have to enjoy what you're doing because retail is very demanding. Holidays are few and far between. Retail involves weekends, it involves nights, but it can be very rewarding. The biggest reward is the feeling that you've accomplished something, that you've given good service, and that you've made a good friend for the company."

■ ■ ■

Let's begin by defining the term *retail*. The United States Census Bureau defines the retail trade sector as businesses that sell items that are usually not transformed in any way; in other words, the buyer is getting a finished product ready for personal use, like a car, a book, or a new outfit. Sales at the retail level are the final step in getting merchandise to the consumer. Retailers are set up to sell merchandise to the general public in small quantities.

Buying goods for resale is what makes retail different from businesses in the agriculture, manufacturing, and construction industries. Farms that sell crops from the point of production are counted in the agriculture sector, not in retail. Likewise, companies that manufacture parts that will be used to build the car you are going to buy are not counted in the retail sector but in the manufacturing sector. But if you decide to purchase a new oil filter for your car, that would be counted as a retail sale. Wholesalers may also buy goods for resale, but they usually are not set up to sell to the general public, and their operations are often set up to sell and deliver merchandise in large quantities.

Another important distinction the Census Bureau makes is between restaurants and grocery stores. Remember how retailers don't really change the product the consumer buys? Well, obviously at a restaurant raw ingredients are transformed on the premises into meals that the customer consumes right then and there. So restaurants and bars are not considered part of the retail trade by the Census Bureau but are in their own category. Thus, the restaurant business is not discussed in this book. Grocery stores are considered part of retail because most of the products the consumer buys are not changed in any way.

The United States Census Bureau divides the retail trade into two main types of retailers:

1. *Store retailers.* A store retailer is exactly what it sounds like: a seller with a fixed location designed to attract a high volume of walk-in traffic. This is still the way most of us buy things. Customers are lured into the store with displays in the windows or by advertising. These retailers include department stores, catalog showrooms, gasoline service stations, automotive dealers, grocery stores, and so on.

2. *Nonstore retailers.* A nonstore retailer has no fixed location for customers to visit for purchases. These

BUSINESSES FOUND
IN THE RETAIL INDUSTRY:

Motor vehicle and parts dealers

Furniture stores

Home furnishings stores

Electronics and appliance stores

Building materials and supplies dealers

Lawn and garden equipment and supplies stores

Food and beverage stores (does not include restaurants)

Health and personal care stores

Gasoline stations

Clothing and clothing accessories stores

Sporting goods, hobby, and musical instrument stores

Book, periodical, and music stores

General merchandise stores

Florists

Office supplies, stationery, and gift stores

Used merchandise stores

Other miscellaneous store retailers

Electronic shopping and mail-order houses

Vending machine operators

Fuel dealers

Other direct selling establishments

businesses include those who sell through the internet, infomercials, direct-response advertising, catalogs, door-to-door selling, in-home demonstrations, and vending machines.

How Important Is the Retail Industry in the U.S. Economy?

The retail industry is such a significant part of the U.S. economy that the Retail Sales Index is considered a leading indicator for the economy. Around the 12th of each month the United States Census Bureau releases a report measuring goods sold in the retail industry. These figures are closely watched as an indication of the state of the economy in the United States.

Some other facts from the Department of Labor regarding the importance of the retail industry are:

- Retail is the second largest industry in the United States, both in number of establishments and number of employees.
- In 2001, the retail industry generated a 9.2 percent share of the nation's total Gross Domestic Product.
- Experts predict that the retail industry will add 2.1 million new jobs between 2002 and 2012, for a total of 17.1 million people employed in retail in 2012.
- Nearly three quarters of workers in the retail industry are employed full time, while approximately one quarter work part time.

- Three of the top 30 occupations expected to yield the highest job growth through 2012 are found in the retail industry—retail salespeople, cashiers, and first-line supervisors/managers of retail sales workers.

While the industry is dominated by small businesses, which account for 95 percent of all businesses, they generate less than 50 percent of all retail store sales.

History of Retail

Retail has been around forever, ever since people have needed things from others to help make life easier or just to survive. People initially acquired goods and services by exchanging them for other goods and services in a process called *barter*, because money hadn't yet been invented. Farmers began to produce extra crops as a means of having items with which to trade. Barter is still used today by many individuals and even some governments. Eventually the first form of money, cattle, was used beginning around the year 9000 B.C. Around the year 1000 B.C., coins were used. Merchants began to travel about acquiring and selling their goods, and the marketplace appeared. Food, pottery, cloth, jewelry, and perfumes were just a few of the items sold.

In ancient Rome, the marketplace, called the forum, was the heart of the city and the center for trade, government, religion, and civic life. At this time, buyers needed to be especially careful about their purchases because it was their responsibility to ensure the quality of the goods they bought. If after the purchase, the buyer discovered the merchandise was inferior, it was pretty much tough luck for the buyer. This is where the Latin saying "caveat emptor," or "let the buyer beware," came from.

As people began to travel and see how others lived in far-away lands, they began to desire the new goods and services they found in these exotic places, such as silks and spices. This desire for other goods and services was so intense that it fueled exploration into unknown and often dangerous territory. For example, the great Venetian explorer Marco Polo traversed the Silk Road to China in the 13th century along with his father and uncle in search of trade opportunities. At the end of the 15th century, Christopher Columbus crossed an unknown ocean in order to find an all-water route to the Orient, so as to more easily obtain the silks and spices that Europeans had come to treasure. Even the Lewis and Clark expedition that began in May 1804 had a trade purpose: to find the elusive all-water route to the Orient.

Retail in America

When the Europeans colonized the Americas, they brought with them the idea of buying and selling goods. Later, the American West provided a unique environment for the development of retail. Here, the trading post, or general store, was born. Not only did the storekeeper offer necessities such as flour, sugar, salt, clothing, tools, dishes, and eggs, but also a center for the community. The storekeeper was one of the most influential and important people in town. He was often the postmaster, and his store served as the post office. He could make arrangements for horse rental. In addition to selling merchandise, he often had to be well versed in the law so as to help townspeople make contracts. The general store sometimes provided meals, or at least a place to come in from the cold and relax for a time around the pot-bellied stove and get caught up on all the news.

Branding

Up until the 20th century, branding was almost nonexistent; sugar was simply sugar. General stores still used mostly the barter system, as farmers did not earn wages for their crops. Sometimes goods were sold on credit. The development of the railroad revolutionized the retail industry and supported the development of specialty stores and department stores because goods from faraway places could be more easily acquired. Merchants began advertising, and store windows were dressed up in an attempt to differentiate one store from all the others. Branding was born.

New Methods of Distribution

In 19th-century America, the majority of the population lived on farms and did not have easy access to stores. Aaron Montgomery Ward came up with a solution for this problem in 1872: the catalog. He published the world's first general merchandise mail-order catalog, with 163 products listed. Ward's idea in founding a mail-order business was to cut the cost of selling products by eliminating the middleman. Ward also started the policy of allowing merchandise to be returned if customers did not find his goods acceptable. His catalog soon became known as "the wish book," and was enjoyed in households all across America. Other retailers, such as Richard Sears, began to copy Ward's idea, and the catalog took a firm hold in American retail history.

The Advent of Shopping
and Changing Attitudes Toward Buyers

At some point, the idea of shopping as a leisure activity was born. Researchers differ greatly in their opinions as to when this trend started. Some feel that it came with the development of big shops, perhaps in Victorian England, where women of means were encouraged to entertain themselves by purchasing things. People began to move from the consumption of necessities in order to survive to a new mentality: living to consume.

As customers began to have choices regarding where they shopped, shrewd business owners came to realize early on that the "customer was king" and that to succeed, excellent customer service was mandatory. Customers who were treated poorly by one establishment simply took their business elsewhere.

The Mall

As a parallel to the invention of the automobile, strip centers began to pop up on the American landscape in the late 1920s, and during the 1950s, the enclosed mall was born. The mall was a place where retail stores, services, and restaurants all came under one roof, complete with parking spaces. The appearance of malls shifted retail from the traditional downtown core out to regional shopping centers. The regional shopping center was one of the most significant changes to American cities in the 20th century. Some megamalls today provide entertainment for customers strolling by, with pianists playing grand pianos, amusement parks, or miniature golf. Sounds like the Roman forum all over again, doesn't it?

Trends in Retail Today

The retail industry evolves as advances in technology, changes in governments, politics, and culture all affect the way business is done. Three important trends in the retail industry today are: category killers, e-commerce, and globalization.

- *Category killers.* Category killers are revolutionizing American retailing. These stores so dominate their retail category that they wind up "killing" the category for everyone else. Examples include Office Depot, PetSmart, Toys "R" Us, Home Depot, Barnes and Noble, and Borders. Small, local stores are often unable to compete and wind up going out of business. Consumers are much more savvy now. Products continue to be lower priced, which means profit margins are shrinking and only the most efficient retailers can survive.

- *E-commerce.* The internet has transformed nearly every aspect of people's lives, including how they shop. Although e-commerce continues to grow, it will supplement other methods of retailing rather than replace them. E-commerce has allowed small businesses to reach new markets.

For large retailers, the key is online/offline integration. For example, if a customer is shopping in a store and can't find the shoes he wants in his size, the employee can immediately search for those shoes online and even have them delivered to the customer's house, if the customer desires. Employees with information technology skills are more desirable than ever.

• *Globalization*. This is the age of the global economy. Much of the supply chain for the retail industry is outside of the United States. Retailers have always been accustomed to worrying about financial issues facing their companies, but as they venture more and more into global markets, they expose themselves to other risks as well, such as currency fluctuations, political instabilities, differing tax rules, and even terrorism. Retailers, like other companies, must be concerned with making a profit for their shareholders or owners. But in this new age, they also need to concern themselves with being good global citizens and minimizing their impact on the environment and the communities in which they operate.

To succeed in this extremely competitive marketplace, retailers will need to make their products more appealing to consumers, rely on powerful branding, and have sophisticated customer management systems and efficient supply chains. Likewise, global retailers will need to have strong risk management policies.

PROFILE
The JCPenney Company

The story of the JCPenney company is a story of the American Dream come true, a rags-to-riches tale in which a small-town young man becomes a retail legend by meeting his customers' needs and providing value for their hard-earned dollars. JCPenney has been in business for over 100 years, weathering two world wars, the Great Depression, and the death of its founder. But perhaps the biggest enemy the company has had to face in recent times is the threat of stagnation.

The history of the company is especially fascinating in that it parallels the history of retail in the United States. James Cash Penney started his business as a partner with two other men in a dry goods and clothing store in Kemmerer, a sleepy frontier mining town in Wyoming. The name of the store was The Golden Rule, and at the time of the store opening, he had to scramble to come up with $2,000 in order to buy into The Golden Rule. In April 1902, the doors opened with Penney running the store.

Amazingly, Penney was able to make a profit in the very first year of operation. Customers were attracted to the business because of his incredible personal service and low prices. For the next few years,

Penney and his partners expanded and opened additional Golden Rule stores. In 1907, Penney was able to buy out his partners.

Unlike his fellow shop owners, Penney recognized that highly skilled employees were key to success in business, and he referred to workers not as employees but as associates. He also believed in sharing the rewards of success and became known for grooming store clerks to become managers as well as partners.

In 1911, sales topped $1 million in 22 stores. In 1913, the company incorporated as J.C. Penney. That same year several partners met in Salt Lake and created the company motto, "Honor, Confidence, Service, and Cooperation," which mirrored the values of management. New managers received a lapel pin engraved with the initials H.C.S.C. in a special ceremony, a tradition that continues to this day. In 1914, the company moved its headquarters to New York City to have easier access to the nation's business center. This move facilitated the buying function as well as transportation and financing.

The company faced national crises along with the country. Those who left the company to serve the nation in World War I were paid a monthly salary of $15, and their jobs were available to them on their return.

Penney made certain the company kept up with advances in the retail industry as they happened. In 1923, visual merchandising became a division within the advertising department. In 1929, a laboratory was established in the New York office to test merchandise to make certain it was fit to be sold in the stores.

While the company weathered the Great Depression, Penney lost his personal fortune. Yet he maintained his commitment to the retail industry. He continued to visit stores. He never was above waiting on customers personally or picking up a broom to clean a store that was not up to his standards. He eventually rebuilt his fortune. James Cash Penney remained at the helm longer than the lifespan of most people, continuing to report for work for a few days each week well into his 90's; he died in 1971 at the age of 95.

But as the JCPenney Company turned 100 years old, it looked old and tired. Net sales in fiscal 2002 and 2003 were below the 2001 level. Now, however, the company has managed to turn things around, and analysts are forecasting record-breaking revenues for 2007.

The aboutface began with new hires in upper management. They were able to steer the company back on course by returning to the hallmark of James Cash Penney's tenure: recognizing the needs of the customer and providing outstanding customer service. Using the latest technology and utilizing the concept of multichannels, that is, integrating all of the channels of distribution—such as stores, web site, and catalog—was critical.

JCPenneys recently installed 35,000 point-of-sale registers to reduce transaction time and give the customer quick and easy access to the company's online merchandise. For example, if a customer purchases baby items, the associate can print out information about decorating the nursery from the company web site. Integrating the store experience with online services provides the best possible customer service. James Cash Penney would be proud.

■ ■ ■

CHAPTER 2

Is Retail
Right for You?

PROFILE

Al Slavin

Wal-Mart, San Antonio, Texas

Those who thrive in the retail industry often share traits in common: outstanding people skills, flexibility, good physical stamina, and the willingness to move wherever the company calls. Al Slavin has demonstrated all of these skills in his retail career and is a highly successful general store manager for a super Wal-Mart in San Antonio, Texas.

He talks about his climb up the corporate ladder. "When I was a senior at Texas A&M, I was working toward a degree in landscape architecture, I had no money, and I had met my future wife. We decided to get married, so I had to get a job. At the time, the landscape architecture field was very depressed; nothing at all was happening. My situation became a matter of surviving. I ended up getting a job at a midsized department store. It wasn't really something I wanted to do, but I had to. I was a manager-trainee. I started to learn about retail, and I realized I had a talent for management. It's more people oriented than you'd think. "

At the same time, Slavin was developing another area of his life as well. "I am an artist at heart. My wife's parents gave me as a gift a two-week study with an artist. I learned more from this guy in two weeks than I had learned in my entire life."

Slavin found that he didn't like the company he was working for, and got a different job. "About a year and a half into it, I switched to a store called Crafts, Etc., as it had an opening for a frame shop manager. With my interest in art, I thought this was the perfect job for me. When I got into that particular store, it was in complete disarray, so I organized it. We completely redid the whole thing, and had the place organized in two weeks. I had a particular method for getting everything organized just so. We quadrupled profits in a few months.

"I ended up moving to Austin, Texas, for this company and opening a new store for them. My art teacher was there as well, so it seemed perfect. But when I got there, I realized that if I wanted to get a house and have kids, I needed a better job, and that's when I went with Wal-Mart. First they moved me to Oklahoma, and then to Oregon and California. I became a store manager in about four years."

The high cost of living in California affected Slavin both on a business level and a personal level. He was managing a store in Gilroy, California. "As a store manager, you've got to keep your people pumped up. We started out in that store making $26 million and went to $30 million in just one year. It was difficult because the expense structure was so high in California.

"Then they put in two new stores on either side of me, 15 miles away in each direction. It destroyed my traffic. So I had to get creative, and when I did, I increased store profit 12 percent. I'd let a company have an RV sale in the parking lot, and my store would get 20 percent of the profits. We also allowed companies to have medical shows in the parking lot. I'd also have sales on merchandise that brought people into the store in droves."

Although the store was doing well, Slavin found the high cost of living quite unappealing and wanted to return to his hometown of San Antonio, Texas. But a transfer was not without cost. "I stepped down to a co-manager position to get back to San Antonio, but eventually I became a store manager again. I've been in my current store for four years. I've grown it from a $94 million store to a $107 million store."

As a store manager, Slavin has two co-managers under him, one responsible for general merchandise and one responsible for food. Each co-manager has an assistant responsible for multiple departments, and under each assistant is a lead person, who is responsible for one department, such as the bakery or the produce area. "It's like having little stores within a store, which is a Sam Walton concept. We have hourly people in charge of million-dollar departments. Electronics in my store does $14 million alone."

Slavin discusses what it takes to succeed in retail. "Retail pays pretty good now. If you are going to pick a job in retail, you need to be able to deal with all kinds of people. Our store has middle-class shoppers as well as grass-roots people with little money or education. Sometimes you have to deal with people who are not nice-mannered. It can be trying.

"We have 50,000–55,000 transactions in this store in just one week. You have to be tolerant because you are dealing with so many people. You also have to have a high energy level, high physical stamina, and be willing to work evenings, weekends, and holidays. If you can't do that, don't even get in there. But there are benefits. "As a manager, I have a lot of opportunity to help people, and that's what keeps me going."

■ ■ ■

This chapter will help you determine if the retail industry is right for you. As Al Slavin discusses in the profile, success in the retail industry calls for a certain skill set. We're going to talk about these skills in detail in this chapter. Probably the most important skill of all is dealing effectively with other people. Good physical stamina, flexibility, and attention to detail are also important. Retail differs from other industries in that many of the businesses in retail are affected by seasonality, which means that retail professionals may work longer hours during certain times of the year.

We're also going to take a look at some retail education programs around the country, and we'll end the chapter with a quiz that helps you inventory your skills and match them to retail jobs.

The information age has empowered customers. Today's customer is more savvy, better educated, more selective about what he or she wants, and much more aware of the many options available when buying. This means the salesperson cannot afford to be rude or indifferent to the customer because the customer can shop elsewhere. Therefore, the salesperson must always be at his or her best and give each customer the best possible service.

Successful retail employees bring three things to encounters with customers. First, the salesperson brings *knowledge* of the products and services available in the store. Coupled with this knowledge is integrity. The salesperson never exaggerates or fabricates details concerning the product, its features, or its warranties. The employee is aware of the competition and researches to keep current.

Secondly, the salesperson makes an effort to truly *understand* the customer's point of view. Listening to the customer is critical to success. Finally, in dealing with the customer, the salesperson brings *patience*, especially when the customer is rude or ill mannered or when the customer does not understand what the salesperson is saying. Successful retailing—and all successful businesses dealings for that matter—are about building *relationships*.

When things go wrong, knowledge, patience, and understanding can go a long way to make things right again. Judith Catherine Duthie, of McNally's Booksellers in Calgary, describes how she handled an unpleasant situation with a customer. "Currently in Calgary, there is a major staff shortage, especially in retail and restaurants. Due to this, our in-store restaurant had to cut back its kitchen hours, serving dinners until a certain point in the evening and then only coffee and baked goods after that.

"The other evening, a gentleman came up to me, asking if I was the manager on duty and to tell me he had a complaint. He had called the store to specifically ask for the restaurant's hours. He was told they were open until 10 P.M. He then walked four blocks (parking in downtown is terrible) only to find the kitchen closed.

"I think the best thing I did in this situation was to sympathize with him and not try to make excuses for the mistake. I apologized heartily for the inconvenience, assured him I would immediately send a blanket e-mail to the staff to make sure it didn't happen to anyone else, thanked him for the feedback, as such comments keep us on our toes when we slip up like this. By the time I offered him a voucher for a free latte, he was smiling and satisfied."

It is also important to dress professionally, regardless of what is currently trendy in the fashion world. The appearance of the employee is the first impression the customer has, and the way the employee is dressed should inspire confidence. Even in stores where employees wear uniforms, it is important they be kept clean—as should shoes. Accessories, such as jewelry, and makeup and hairstyles, should also be appropriate for the environment. Management should set the example.

Dealing with the public boils down to one word: respect. The outstanding employee communicates respect to the customer, regardless of the customer's age, socioeconomic status, education, or language.

Seasonality

Seasonality is one of the hallmarks of the retail industry. And within the industry, the busy season varies from business to business. For the majority of retailers, the busiest season is the last quarter of the year, October through December, due to the Christmas holidays. Retailers start receiving extra merchandise for the season as early as September, and many stay open extra hours between the Thanksgiving and Christmas holidays. The busiest day of the year for many retailers is Black Friday, the day after Thanksgiving. Black Friday is so-named because stores are in the black, meaning they are making money rather than losing it, which is called in the red.

Judith Catherine Duthie, of McNally Robinson Booksellers, talks about her store's Christmas rush. "Christmas is an incredibly busy season. Christmas is helping out customer after customer after customer. You get into the store and literally don't stop for eight hours. Lots of book recommendations flying. Lots of publishers bring out books this time of year, so all the new books are coming out. Then the awards are coming up, and everyone is trying to read the winners and the runners-up. In January, things settle down as far as customers are concerned, but there's lots of footwork to do, with sending back books that didn't sell. January and February are much calmer, and are more about taking care of the store."

Duthie says in the book-selling business, another busy season is the summer. "Then in summer, we have more customers again. People are looking for beach reads, those nice, light, don't-make-me-think-too-hard books that allow them to take a break from reality."

According to the Census Bureau, department stores average 15 percent of their entire year's sales in December, while jewelry stores average a whopping 24 percent for December alone. However, the busy season is different for other businesses. The busiest holiday for florists is Valentine's Day. For hardware stores, building materials and supplies stores, and motor vehicle dealers, which have sales more evenly spread throughout the year, the busiest time is the second quarter, April through June. This makes sense when you consider that more homes are sold in the spring, and home repairs are usually done in warmer months. Businesses selling everyday necessities such as food and gas are not quite as affected by seasonality as other businesses.

For those working in retail, seasonality means that employees usually are not allowed to take vacation during the busy time. On the plus side, seasonality can also translate into more opportunities for those seeking to break into a particular business. Retail employment typically swells during the holiday season, and the demand isn't just for cashiers and salespeople. During the busy seasons, large retail stores also need people for stocking, pricing, tagging, driving, and cleaning.

RETAIL WORKER'S LIFE IN THE 19TH CENTURY

"The store must be open from 6:00 A.M. to 9:00 P.M. the year round. Men employees are given one evening a week for courting, and two if they go to prayer meeting. After 14 hours of work in the store, the leisure hours should be spent mostly in reading."

(From a 19th-century retail establishment's *Instruction to Employees*)

Long Hours

The hours for retail employees have improved dramatically since the 19th century. Most hourly workers work a standard 40-hour workweek, and if they work longer, they are usually paid overtime. Managers and other salaried workers, including those who work at corporate headquarters, work an average of 40–50 hours per week. But during the busy season or during a special sale, they may work longer. And for those who own their own businesses, the hours can be longer yet. New business owners may put in anywhere from 10 to 16 hours per day.

Physical Stamina

Most of the jobs in retail, and certainly all of the in-store jobs, require tremendous physical stamina. Sales associates spend most of the day on their feet, and many of the positions require sales associates to move boxes from the stock room to the sales floor for restocking. Store managers constantly walk the store to make sure everything is perfect. Loss prevention associates walk the floors in an attempt to cut down on shoplifting. Visual merchants may need the most physical stamina of all, because they create window displays with heavy props or rearrange entire departments. There is no doubt that retail calls for people who are energetic and ready to meet the physical demands of the industry.

Flexibility

Retail businesses are under tremendous pressure to keep costs down in order to turn a profit and stay in business. For many establishments, labor costs can be the single highest expense. Businesses try to maintain just the right number of employees on the floor. If too many are scheduled, labor costs can sky-rocket. If too few are scheduled, customers do not get good service and shoplifting may increase.

Workplace flexibility refers to both the employer and the employee thinking innovatively about the workweek. Retail salespeople's schedules often change from week to week to accommodate the needs of the store. Retail managers must keep these costs in check, and still ensure that store personnel will be able to provide outstanding customer service.

Attention to Detail

There is an old expression in retail, "Retail is in the detail." This means that the best retail associates are concerned with what may seem like the smallest details to the rest of us. This attention to detail may mean the difference between a great in-store experience for the customers and a mediocre one. Oftentimes, even a single fixture in a store can tell a whole story to a customer. Are the products arranged neatly on the fixtures so that the customer can find what he or she is looking for? If the fixture is holding clothing, is it arranged by size? Are the garments crisp and fresh looking? If the fixture is holding other merchandise such as DVDs, or books, is the fixture spotlessly clean? Is inventory constantly replenished? If the merchandise is not out on the floor and arranged so that the customer can find it, then it can't be sold.

Specialty Expertise

Retail is an industry where you can sell a wide variety of merchandise or specialize and become an expert in just one area. Developing an area of expertise often leads to the sales associate making more money. For example, many people who work in retail jewelry train to become gemologists. Associates working in the automotive, appliance, or computer fields need to be completely knowledgeable about all the features of the products they sell. Expertise in an area inspires confidence in the customer and can help to attract business.

Training and Education

Do you need a college education in order to work in the retail industry? The definitive answer is: maybe, maybe not. It all depends on the area in which you wish to work and on the company you have targeted. Al Slavin, a general store manager for a super Wal-Mart, discusses a great hire he made some years back. "I actually hired a maintenance man some years ago; he's a store manager now. He was an immigrant from Chile, and had been a chef. I liked him immediately because he was smiling, he was confident in his abilities, he was personable, and he had this great attitude. He told me when I hired him, 'I can do this job—I will do the work of three men.' I'd heard that one before, but this guy delivered. Whenever I asked him to do something, even the most unpleasant task, he never missed a beat. He worked hard, he had excellent people skills, and he was smart. So here at Wal-Mart, you can start off as a janitor, and you could wind up being a VP or a store manager. We recognize talent."

You will occasionally hear stories of individuals so talented that they were able to enjoy professional success without a college education. Clearly, you don't have to have a college degree in order to succeed in many areas of retail.

But there is also no doubt that a college degree makes everything happen faster, such as getting in the door and getting promoted. A college degree definitely earns you more money to start and, most likely, more money in the long run. The United States Department of Commerce reports that adults age 18 and over with a bachelor's degree earned an average of $50,623 a year in 2001, compared with those with just a high school diploma, who earned an average of $26,795. That comes out to $23,828 more per year for college graduates. Advanced degree-holders made even more, with an average yearly income of $72,869. And of course, there are certain positions and companies for which a college degree is mandatory, such as accounting and in many companies, management.

What if you have a college degree, but it's in another field of study besides business, a field like liberal arts? Don't worry. Many employers actually welcome a liberal arts degree combined with excellent communication skills and computer

FIGURE 2.1: **EMPLOYERS RATE THE IMPORTANCE OF CANDIDATE QUALITIES/SKILLS**

Rated on a 5-point scale: 1 = Not at all important and
5 = Extremely important

Communication skills	4.7
Honesty/integrity	4.7
Teamwork skills	4.6
Strong work ethic	4.5
Analytical skills	4.4
Flexibility/adaptability	4.4
Interpersonal skills	4.4
Motivation/initiative	4.4
Computer skills	4.3
Detail-oriented	4.1
Organizational skills	4.1
Leadership skills	4.0
Self-confidence	4.0

Source: *Job Outlook 2006*, National Association of Colleges and Employers.

literacy. Employers are looking for candidates who are bright, well-rounded, and have some practical experience. Students who have no practical experience and very specialized degrees will have greater difficulty finding jobs.

According to a 2006 study by the National Association of Colleges and Employers (NACE), employers report that they consider strong communications skills to be the single most important attribute a candidate can have, and also the one most lacking among candidates. See Figure 2.1 on how other traits are ranked.

The candidate's grade point average also determines whether or not a company is interested in interviewing a candidate. More than half of the companies in the study in Figure 2.1 reported that they want candidates with a GPA of 3.0 or higher.

Educational Opportunities in Retail

Where can you get an education that will prepare you for a career in retail? Although many colleges and universities offer degree programs specifically aimed at the retail industry, others offer a certificate program that complements other fields of study, such as marketing or economics.

Below is a sampling of the many programs available:

- **Fashion Schools**
  - *The Fashion School at Kent State* (www.thefashion school.kent.edu), Kent, Ohio. The Fashion School offers a bachelor of science in fashion merchandising as well as a bachelor of arts in fashion design. The program offers a strong liberal arts foundation joined with an industry-focused major in fashion. A five-year MBA in fashion merchandising is available. Internships are a part of the program.

- *The Fashion Institute of Design and Merchandising* (www.fidm.com), four locations in California. FIDM, with 5,500 full-time students, offers an associate of arts degree, professional designation, and advanced study degree programs in fashion design, merchandise marketing, product development, textile design, merchandising and marketing, etc.

- **Retailing**
  - *The University of Arizona* (www.cals.arizona.edu/fcs /tlc/), Tucson, Arizona. The University of Arizona's program in retailing and consumer sciences (RCSC) offers both four-year and graduate studies leading to BS, MS, and PhD degrees. Internships with major retailers are available.
  - *Georgia Southern University* (coba.georgiasouthern .edu/centers/crs/main.htm), Statesboro, Georgia. The Center serves business majors through a BBA in marketing with an emphasis in retail store management or marketing with an emphasis in fashion merchandising. Retail point of sale is offered as a second discipline to students majoring in information systems.
  - *Santa Clara University Retail Management Institute* (www.scu.edu/rmi/index.html), Santa Clara, California. The Institute provides opportunities for students and retail professionals through three major programs, and is open to undergraduates in every field who are interested in retailing careers. There is

also a management development program, as well as the Retail Workbench Research and Education Center, which is the Institute's retail research program.

- *University of Florida* (www.cba.ufl.edu/mkt/crer/), Gainesville, Florida. The Miller Center for Retailing Education and Research is for students interested in careers in retailing, individuals currently in retailing seeking continuing education, retailers and academics who want to understand each other's concerns, and research on retailing issues.
- *Florida State University* (www.fsu.edu), Tallahassee, Florida. FSU offers graduate programs in clothing, textiles, and merchandising, with an emphasis in apparel product development and retail merchandising.
- *Michigan State University* (www.hed.msu.edu/inter nationalretailing/program/index.html), East Lansing, Michigan. MSU offers a merchandising management major focusing on the retail industry as part of its international retailing program.

- **Marketing**
  - *The University of Texas at Austin* (www.mccombs .utexas.edu/), Austin, Texas. Offers courses in supply chain management, information systems, marketing research, and marketing.
  - *The Kellogg School of Management of Northwestern University,* (www.kellogg.northwestern.edu/mar keting/index.htm), Evanston, Illinois. Offers two

marketing majors: marketing and marketing management. Marketing management prepares students for careers in retailing, entrepreneurship, packaged goods, and e-commerce. The marketing department is rated at the top in national and international ranking surveys during the last 15 years.

Many other programs are available. Check with your local university to see if they have a program. Typically, they do.

Quiz

One of the great things about the retail industry is that there's room for people with many different skill sets. Ask yourself the following questions, and then take a look at Figures 2.2 and 2.3. (Figure 2.2 lists skills needed for each retail position discussed in this book. Look closely at the positions requiring your skills. Then take a look Figure 2.3, which describes the working conditions for each position.) Then read Chapters 3 and 4, which describe in detail the jobs listed in the charts.

1. Are you willing to work a schedule that changes from week to week?
2. Would you work nights, weekends, and holidays?
3. Do you enjoy interacting with new people every day?
4. Do you enjoy helping people meet their shopping needs?
5. Is money of prime importance to you?
6. Do you have strong people skills?

7. Do you have strong analytical skills?
8. Do you have strong fashion sense?
9. Are you creative?
10. Do you have plenty of physical stamina?
11. Do you like to lead?
12. Are you willing to travel?

FIGURE **2.2: SKILLS NEEDED FOR THE JOBS LISTED**

JOB TITLE	College Education	People Skills	Analytical Skills	Physical Stamina	Creative Skills
Salesperson	Not necessary	Outstanding	Moderate	High	Good
Salesperson Supervisor	A good idea	Outstanding	Good	High	Moderate
Loss Prevention	A good idea	Good	Good to high	High	Good
Visual Merchants	Not necessary	Moderate	Moderate	Extremely high	Extremely high
Buyer	A good idea	Good	High	Good	High
Marketing	Usually required	Good	High	Good	High
Marketing Research	Usually required	Good	Extremely high	Good	High
Accounting & Finance	Usually required	Good	Extremely high	Good	Moderate
Information Technology	Usually required	Good	Extremely high	Good	Moderate
Store Development	Usually required	Good	High	High	High

FIGURE 2.3: WORKING CONDITIONS

	Travel Required	Earnings	Is There Seasonality?	Must Work Flexible Hours	Must Work Nights, Weekends	Average Number of Hours Worked
Salesperson	Not usually	Modest, unless you work for commission	Yes	Yes	Yes	40
Salesperson Supervisor	Not usually	Average; but some store managers can make six figures	Yes	Yes	Yes	40 plus
Loss Prevention	Not usually	Good	Yes	Yes	Yes	40 plus
Visual Merchants	Not usually	Good	Yes	Yes	Sometimes	40 plus
Buyer	Some	Good	Yes	Fixed schedule	Rarely	40 plus
Marketing	Some	Good to very good	Not as much as an in-store job	Fixed schedule	Rarely	40 plus
Marketing Research	Some	Good to very good	Not as much as an in-store job	Fixed schedule	Rarely	40 plus
Accounting and Finance	Not Usually	Good to very good	Yes	Fixed schedule	Rarely	40 plus
IT	Not usually	Good to very good	Not as much as an in-store job	Fixed schedule	Sometimes	40 plus
Store Development	Yes, as much as 30–40%	Good to very good	Not as much as an in-store job	Sometimes	Sometimes	40 plus

Jobs
in the Store

PROFILE

Judith Catherine Duthie

McNally Robinson Booksellers
Calgary, Alberta, Canada

Judith Catherine Duthie's love affair with books began when she was a child. "I really got into reading when I was in the fourth grade, when a teacher I had read aloud classics to us. I can still remember the scenes in my head that formed while she was reading."

Now, as a salesperson at McNally Robinson Booksellers in Calgary, Canada, Duthie has the opportunity to share her love of books with the customers who come in to shop. "I was in drama in university, but then I went over to literature. I love the world of books, and I love the worlds inside of them.

"I got started selling books when I was in university. I went into an independent, very tiny bookstore that had maybe 300 to 400 square feet. And I thought, 'This would be a great job while I finish university.' And I went to work there, and that's when I fell in love with bookselling."

Duthie worked at that store until she graduated, and then moved over to McNally Robinson Booksellers, a small independent chain with locations in Winnipeg, Saskatoon, Calgary, and New York City.

Duthie thoroughly enjoys helping customers. "When a customer comes into the store and asks for a recommendation, I ask the customer, 'What was a book that you read and loved?' And then it's like a spider web in my mind, and I start making connections and pulling books off the shelves, and I discuss these choices with the customer. You sort of encourage the customer to pick their own book, and really what you are doing is helping them to narrow it down to something they are likely to enjoy.

"We have a lot of repeat customers. One of the joys of bookselling is when a customer comes back in the store, and they say,

'You recommended this book to me. Can you give me another?' It's more of a friendship than anything. And sometimes the regular customers will start selling to you. It's almost a two-way street. Our favorite question is, 'What are you reading now?'"

Besides helping customers out with recommendations, Duthie has other sales duties as well. "We have the store divided up into sections. I'm in charge of the romance section and the interior design section. Each week, I track the sales of everything that's sold in those sections. Then I say, 'We sold six of this book, I'd better order some more.' This is something that doesn't happen with the big chain bookstores. Their staffs don't have as much say as to what happens in the store because the chains have so many jobs centralized.

"I also work at the desk, taking money, and shelving books and straightening up. A lot of the time is taken up with the customers, and I will place special orders for books that are not in the store. One of my favorite parts of my job is researching those special orders.

"We also have to make returns of books to the publishers of those books that didn't sell well in our store. We have many author events in the store.

"I also like working the register, because then I get to see what people are buying, and I talk to the customers. For example, if someone is buying a book by Bernard Cornwell, I tell them, 'If you are reading Cornwell, you might also enjoy reading Jack Whyte.'"

And every now again, a customer approaches Duthie's register bearing one of the classics Duthie's fourth grade teacher first read to her. "When people bring these books to me, I remember once again how wonderful they really are."

■ ■ ■

Duthie does a fantastic job of describing the perfect salesperson in her profile: someone who brings a passion for the merchandise to the job, as well as someone who enjoys working with people. In this chapter, we're going to delve deeper into retail jobs in a store environment, including salespeople, managers, loss prevention associates, and visual merchants. For each of these jobs, we'll describe the duties involved, the qualifications, employment outlook, and earnings.

Retail Salespeople

The salesperson is the most important member of the retail team because this is the person who will have direct contact with the customer. No matter how clever the ad campaign, how terrific the window displays look, or how cool the merchandise is, all it takes is one rude, slovenly, or incompetent salesperson to make a customer decide to never do business in the store again. The efforts of the entire retail team can be ruined by one bad salesperson. In the same vein, the salesperson who provides outstanding customer service may win a friend for the company for years to come.

The Good News and Things to Consider

Retail sales positions are expected to grow by 14 percent through the year 2014, making this career the 13th-fastest growing career in the United States, translating to a whopping 1.35 million new jobs. Jobs open up fairly easily because many workers leave the occupation each year. If you have excellent people skills, enjoy helping people find products that serve their needs, have tact, patience, a neat appearance, an interest in sales work, and the ability to communicate clearly, this may be the job for you. If you are looking for part-time work, retail sales may also be the place for you; one quarter of the employees in this industry work part time.

Most salespeople work weekends and evenings, and put in extra time during peak retail periods such as Christmas. So planning an extended vacation during the Thanksgiving and Christmas holidays may not be possible. Many times the schedule changes from week to week.

So What Does a Retail Salesperson Do?

The retail salesperson's most important tasks are to assist the customer in finding what he or she is looking for and to try to interest the customer in buying the merchandise. The sales-person must know the stock, be able to describe a product's features, demonstrate its use, and know what's on hand. If the merchandise is particularly complex, the salesperson may need special knowledge or training. For example, those selling cars must be able to explain all the features of all the different models, the financing available, and the guarantees.

It is imperative that salespeople provide courteous and efficient customer service. Even when customers are rude, patience and courtesy are required. If a customer wants an item that is not on the sales floor, the salesperson may check the stock room, call another location, or even place an order for the merchandise.

Most salespeople not only help the customers find what they are looking for but also ring up the sale as well. This involves taking payment in the form of cash, credit or debit cards, or checks. Then the salesperson gives a receipt and change, if necessary, and bags or packs the purchase.

The salesperson may have to open or close a register. Closing out the register is a much more involved process than opening, because it's necessary to count up all the cash, sepa-rate the charge slips, coupons, and vouchers, and then turn everything in to the main office. If the salesperson has too many shortages, this could be cause for dismissal.

Other tasks the salesperson may handle include taking care of merchandise returns and exchanges, wrapping gifts, and general cleaning, such as dusting. Salespeople also help bring out new merchandise and stock the shelves or the racks. They may arrange for the mailing of customer purchases, take inventory, and sometimes help prepare displays. If there is a special promotion or sale on the merchandise, the salesperson must be aware of it. A good salesperson also looks out for security risks and theft and knows how to handle or prevent such situations.

Working Conditions

Working in a retail establishment is generally pleasant because stores are heated and cooled, clean, and well lighted. Still, some salespeople do work outside selling plants in a nursery, lumber, or even cars.

The workweek for those in retail almost always includes weeknights, weekends, and some holidays. Retailers always seem to be preparing for "the big sale." Christmas inventory arrives in most large stores in September, and it is difficult to get vacation from Thanksgiving right through to the beginning of January.

Qualifications

The good news about sales positions is that there are usually no formal education requirements, although most employers prefer a high school diploma or the equivalent. Probably the most important asset a sales candidate can have is the ability to deal with the public. Good salespeople are friendly and tactful, and can handle even the most difficult customers.

Employers also look for candidates with neat appearances. A candidate who can speak more than one language in a bilingual community is also an asset to the company.

Before hiring a salesperson, some employers conduct background checks. In small stores, training is usually on the job, while larger companies may have someone from the personnel department conduct a more formal training program on how to operate the registers. These formal training programs may also include discussions on customer service, security, and store policies and procedures. Occasionally large department stores allow additional training to be given by manufacturers' representatives.

For example, the manufacturer of a line of lady's handbags may explain to the employees in the handbag department about the fabrics and materials used in the bag, which could be selling points when dealing with customers. Many stores have periodic training for all employees so that they can continually update and improve their skills, with special emphasis on customer service.

Getting Ahead

As salespeople gain experience and seniority, they usually move ahead to positions of greater responsibility. Getting ahead in a small store may be more difficult, simply because the one and only manager, the owner, does most of the managerial work. Large retail businesses often hire college graduates as manager-trainees, so getting ahead in large companies may require a college education. With that said, truly out-standing individuals without a college education can advance in some companies.

Employment Outlook

The outlook for retail sales jobs is expected to be good, and the United States Department of Labor expects jobs to grow about as fast as the average for all occupations throughout the year 2014. Jobs are found all over the United States because retail establishments are found in every city and town. Employment is distributed in much the same pattern as is the population.

When the economy is good, retail opportunities abound because people have the disposable income needed to buy costly items such as cars, appliances, and furniture. During economic downturns, sales for non-necessities decline and so does the need for salespeople. Because turnover among retail salespeople is high, the employer often does not actually lay existing employees off. Instead, the employer may simply not replace those who leave.

How Much Do Salespeople Make?

Many retail sales positions start out paying the minimum wage, which was $5.85 per hour in the year 2007 in most states. Some states, such as California and Maine, have a higher minimum wage. Starting pay may also be higher in areas where there is little unemployment. According to the Bureau of Labor Statistics, median hourly earnings, including commissions, for all retail salespeople were $8.98 per hour in May 2004.

The median hourly earnings by industry within retail for May 2004:

Automobile dealers	$ 18.61
Building materials and supplies dealers	10.85
Department stores	8.47
Other general merchandise stores	8.36
Clothing stores	8.17

Benefits

Benefits in large establishments are comparable to those offered by other employers, but may be limited in small retail businesses. One of the best benefits is the employee discount, which enables the salesperson to purchase merchandise in the store at a discount.

WHAT'S COMMISSION?

Under a commission system, salespeople receive a percentage of the sales they generate. This system is often used with big ticket items, such as electronics, furniture, men's suits, and jewelry. The commission system allows salespeople to increase their earnings considerably. Some in sales earn up to $30,000 or more per year in commissions.

PROFILE
Deb Comeau
Keepsake Quilting, The Lakes Region, New Hampshire

Being a manager at one of the largest quilt shops on the planet is Deb Comeau's idea of the perfect blend of business and pleasure. Comeau has been a part of Keepsake Quilting, located in the Lakes Region of New Hampshire, for more than five years. She came to the job with plenty of business experience as well as a degree in marketing, and in addition, she is an accomplished quilter. "Quilting is more than a hobby for me. It's an obsession. When we moved here from Massachusetts, I told my husband that if a job opened up at Keepsake, it would be perfect."

A job did open up, and today Comeau manages three stores for the company, including Keepsake Quilting, Patternworks, and Keepsake NeedleArts. "Patternworks features yarns from all over the world. The world of fibers has expanded. We have everything from the fibers that you used to use, to new, creative, funky yarns that you can do a lot with. Knitting is coming back, and has caught on big with college-age kids, so that's a good thing."

As a manager, Comeau makes certain she is aware of such trends and thinks of ways to get people into the shops. "I manage the shops and the employees within those shops. I need to figure out what it's going to take to get people in and spend money. People have only so much disposable income. Right now we are planning a weekend retreat for quilters, and at the end of the weekend, you will have a completed project.

"We also schedule special shows in the store, and sometimes designers lend out their wares. Bus tours have also been a key part of the business. Groups will book a bus that usually averages 50 ladies, and we must make certain we have enough staff to accommodate these customers. And then there are the leaf peepers, people who love to come to the area for the fall, see the beautiful leaves and then shop with us.

"Some people have a lifelong dream of coming to Keepsake Quilting, which is like the Disney World of quilting and shopping. We not only get bus tours from New York, Pennsylvania, Massachusetts, but also from England, Ireland, Australia, and all over the world. There is so much gratification in seeing their reaction to the store. They are amazed by the selection, as we carry over 10,000 bolts of fabric, while the average quilt store carries fewer than 1,000. It's much more than they expect.

"That in and of itself is an awesome thing to see, but you want to make every person's shopping experience a unique experience.

Definitely customer service is the key. The owners who started this company knew that. You can go on the internet today and buy fabric, but here you get a human being to help you out, to pick out the fabrics with you and get the right colors. Our employees are quilters, and they know their industry. It's such an upbeat environment."

And of course as a manager, Comeau's duties include hiring employees. She discussed what she looks for in a potential employee. "I look for someone who works with customers in a very positive way. For example, how do you deal with someone who wants to make a project that is a bit too complicated without insulting the person? You've got to be a people person and step up to the challenge."

Comeau says that she spends about half of her time on the floor with customers and the other half behind the scenes. She has only one complaint, the same complaint that everyone in the store has. "We all wish there were more hours in the day!"

Retail Store Managers

Simply put, the retail store manager supervises the sales force. But exactly what does that mean? The manager's real job is to get the best out of each resource available for the good of the company. The manager must inspire the sales force to provide outstanding customer service and grooms exceptional salespeople to advance within the company, training them in every facet of the business. At the same time, the manager prepares for his or her own advancement by learning new skills and expanding the knowledge base. The effective manager communicates with customers and learns about their wants and desires and relays this information to corporate, keeping buyers abreast of market trends in his or her particular community. There may be many levels of managers within one store, especially large ones.

The Good News and Things to Consider

In many businesses, managers are promoted from within the company, so if you are already working as a salesperson, you may have an advantage. If you already have a college degree, many companies will consider hiring you in as a manager-trainee. Overall growth for these supervisory positions is projected to grow more slowly than average. Managers still must work evenings, weekends, and holidays, with some managers working more than 40 hours per week.

So What Does a Retail Manager Do?

Managers are responsible for supervising the employees in their department. Their duties depend on the size of their department and the management philosophy of the company. For example, in a small store, there might be only one manager overseeing all functions in the store, from buying the merchandise to advertising to inventory control. This is a common scenario in privately owned businesses.

In large retail establishments with many workers, there can be many layers of managers. In department stores, one manager may be in charge of a single department, such as costume jewelry, and oversee several salespeople. This manager may report to an area manager, who is in charge of a group of departments, such as costume jewelry, accessories, and handbags. The area manager might report to one of several assistant store managers, who in turn report to the general manager of the store.

A grocery store is likely to have a produce manager and a meat manager who report to the store manager; an auto dealership may have associates reporting to a sales manager. A manager may responsible for the interviewing, hiring, and training of employees, as well as preparing the work schedule and assigning specific duties to each worker. Managers often handle customer complaints and ensure that customers are receiving outstanding service. They may also handle purchasing, budgeting, and accounting.

The overall job of these managers is to make certain that their areas run smoothly, and they direct employees to stock shelves, clean and organize the merchandise, price and ticket the goods, and take inventory. Sometimes managers greet and wait on customers.

Working Conditions

Many retail sales managers have offices, generally inside the store. Lower level managers may have informal offices in the stock rooms of the department(s) they manage. Many of these managers estimate that they spend about half of their time doing paperwork and the other half either working on the sales floor supervising employees or actually waiting on customers.

Managers generally work at least a 40-hour week, and sometimes longer. It can be difficult to get time off during the critical holiday season, and just like salespeople, managers are expected to work weeknights, weekends, and during big store sales.

What Are the Qualifications?

Retail managers learn much of what they know through work experience. Many managers start out as salespeople and gain the experience necessary to manage others. They learn the policies of the company, how to provide exemplary customer service, and merchandising.

Companies differ on educational requirements for their managers, and those requiring a college education for management positions vary on the preferred area of study. Generally, courses in accounting, marketing, management, sales, psychology, sociology, and communication are recommended. Managers must also be competent with computers in order to use the cash registers, inventory control systems, and other documentation.

Managers may have degrees in liberal arts, social sciences, business, or management. Many companies allow college students to intern in their companies to gain experience and to allow the student to determine if retail is a career of interest.

Once employed, managers are usually trained in a variety of areas, from interviewing and hiring to customer service skills, scheduling, and inventory management. Some companies prefer to rotate managers through several departments, and sometimes through different store locations as well. Large retailers usually have extensive programs covering all areas of their operation. College graduates are usually able to enter these training programs directly.

Managers must possess outstanding people skills. They need to be able to direct and motivate the sales force. Managers need to be decisive, flexible, and self-disciplined, and to exhibit good judgment. They must be able to deal with all sorts of customers, including the difficult and demanding. They must also possess the skills needed to inspire their sales staff to be motivated and organized. Managers should groom salespeople to rise to the next level.

Large companies often have career ladder programs. Managers may be expected to transfer within the company from one store to another in order to gain the skills necessary to move to the next level. This may mean that managers have to relocate in order to advance. Advancement is usually more difficult in small companies where there isn't much turnover.

Employment Outlook

In 2004, sales supervisors numbered 2.2 million. Approximately 36 percent were self-employed, as most were store owners. Another 43 percent were wage and salary workers employed in the retail sector. Some of the largest employers were grocery stores, department stores, motor vehicle and parts dealers, and clothing and clothing accessory stores. The remaining sales supervisors worked in nonretail establishments.

For people interested in retail management positions, those with backgrounds in retail have the best chance at securing a supervisory position. Candidates can expect competition for management positions.

Employment of retail sales managers is expected to grow more slowly than average for all occupations through the year 2014. Job openings will occur as experienced supervisors get promoted, transfer into other occupations, and leave the work force all together. However, job turnover is somewhat low.

How Much Do Managers Make?

Earnings vary wildly depending on the size of the company, geographic region, level of responsibility of the position, and background.

According to the Bureau of Labor Statistics, in May 2004, the median annual earnings of salaried supervisors of retail sales workers, including commissions, were $32,720. Within the industry, there was considerable variation by sector:

Building materials and supplies dealers	$ 34,210
Grocery stores	31,360
Clothing stores	30,660
Other general merchandise stores	30,150
Gasoline stations	27,510

Sometimes managers receive commission as well as salaries, perhaps a percentage of the department or store sales. If sales meet or exceed targets, managers may receive a bonus or other awards. Many upper level mangers in retail stores earn six figures.

Loss Prevention Careers

Loss prevention employees deal with the disappearance of merchandise and/or money in retail stores. Retailers keep track of merchandise as it comes into the store, and most retailers do a physical inventory, usually twice a year, to see what's still in the store. The difference between what came in and what should still be on the shelves is called shrinkage. Shrinkage is caused by shoplifting, employee theft, paperwork error on the part of employees, or vendor fraud. Security experts are of the opinion that the in-store thief is responsible for at least 50 percent of shrinkage. See Figure 3.1.

Successful loss prevention programs prevent theft, stopping it before it happens. Al Slavin, a general store manager for Wal-Mart in San Antonio, Texas, discussed how his store is handling the problem of shrinkage. "Theft is an issue for every store. We try to combat it using aggressive hospitality. That means we go up to someone who is acting suspiciously, and greet that person. 'Hi, how are you doing? Can I help you? Are you finding what you need?' The idea is to let that person know that he or she has been recognized, and hopefully, deter the theft.

"We have professionals on all levels. We had a lady come in, dump merchandise out of one box, and fill up that empty box with $3,000 worth of DVDs. Thieves come in with baby strollers and put merchandise beneath the baby.

"We do have people who actually walk around watching, and we used to call this *loss prevention*. But now we call them *asset protection managers*. These people actually spend a lot more time now going through paperwork looking for areas of mismanagement, such as missed markdowns. Shrinkage in the company is somewhere between $1–1.5 billion."

According to the latest National Retail Security Survey report on retail theft, shrinkage cost U.S. retailers over $37 billion in 2005. Inventory shrinkage remains the single largest category of larceny in the United States, more than motor vehicle theft, bank robbery, and household burglary combined.

Shrinkage hurts everyone, not just retailers. Retailers pass on the cost of lost goods to the consumer, who winds up paying higher prices. Thieves also tend to steal hot-selling items, which means that those items are less likely to be on the store shelves when the consumer goes shopping for them.

FIGURE **3.1**: **INVENTORY SHRINKAGE**

Source of Inventory Shrinkage	% of Loss	$ Lost (in billions)
Employee Theft	47	$ 17.6
Shoplifting	33	$ 12.3
Administrative Error	15	$ 5.5
Vendor Fraud	5	$ 1.9
Total Inventory Shrinkage		$ 37.4

Source: National Retail Security Survey, final report for 2005 (based on 2005 retail sales and inventory shrinkage).

So What Does a Loss Prevention Associate Do?

Depending on the level of the associate, the loss prevention employee may be involved with security technologies such as antishoplifting devices, digital video, and point-of-sale systems to help identify sources of theft. The newest security technologies involve point-of-sale software that detects potential theft problems at the cash register. Using this software, loss prevention personnel are able to note who sold what to whom with a click of the button. Another new item is a tiny antitheft label the size of a paper clip that is placed inside a product or package where it is hidden from view.

It is a known fact that retailers who actively use security technologies have less overall shrinkage than those who do not.

Loss prevention personnel often have the following duties:

- conduct surveillance to detect and apprehend shoplifters,
- conduct routine inspections of the facility to maintain physical security and protection of assets,
- monitor closed circuit television systems,
- enforce company standards as they relate to security and safety procedures,
- participate in the training of new hire associates in matters of loss prevention,
- conduct daily, weekly, and monthly store audits,
- ensure physical security by controlling access of associates and visitors, along with maintaining visitor control logs,

- conduct safety inspections and communicate hazards to supervisor on duty, and
- participate in the store's loss prevention and safety programs.

Loss prevention managers at higher levels
- manage all the loss prevention activities for all the stores in a district or region,
- manage a company loss prevention awareness program within the region designed to educate, empower, and reward employees for their shrink reduction efforts,
- create and manage budgets,
- participate in new store openings,
- investigate stores with unusually high shrinkage issues, and
- serve as liaison with law enforcement and the legal community.

Working Conditions

Loss prevention employees need to work the same hours as other retail store employees, so they work evenings, weekends, and some holidays. Theft is especially rampant during crowded holiday shopping times, so these are especially busy times.

What Are the Qualifications?

Probably the most important skill a loss prevention associate can have is the ability to perceive situations accurately. It is imperative to handle difficult situations with diplomacy and

FIGURE **3.2: LOSS PREVENTION MEDIAN INCOMES**

Loss Prevention Positions	New York, NY	Los Angeles, CA	Dallas, TX
Representative	$ 32,163	$ 30,719	$ 27,753
Director	$144,897	$138,391	$125,027

Source: Salary.com

to maintain a fair and consistent set of standards. Loss prevention associates need to have outstanding communication skills and should be able to provide documentation and maintain records. Loss prevention employees also need to be physically fit, because the job may call for extended periods of standing. Excellent hearing and vision are also required.

How Much Do Loss Prevention Associates Make?

Salaries vary greatly by geographic region, and they tend to be higher in cities with higher costs of living. See Figure 3.2.

Visual Merchant

Have you ever seen a store window that was so incredible that you just had to go inside the store and take a look around? And then when you got inside, the merchandise was displayed so beautifully that you wound up buying something even though you hadn't planned on making a purchase? More than likely a visual merchandiser had been hard at work, creating displays so appealing that customers were irresistibly drawn to the merchandise.

PROFILE

Mindy Miles Greenberg
Visual Merchant,
New York, New York

The visual merchant sounds more like that of magician: someone who transforms the ordinary into the extraordinary, casting a spell over customers through enchanting window displays that lure them into the store to make a purchase.

Mindy Miles Greenberg, a top visual merchant in the New York City area, explains just what a visual merchant can do. "A visual merchant takes a garment from a box that sits in the store and does magic to the garment and makes it sell. When it's shipped, the garment arrives looking like a rag or a dirty towel, and you iron everything, and you give it whatever shape it doesn't have by pinning. You fluff it, and you put it on the mannequin or the wall display, making it look like a million bucks. Then it looks like everybody's dream. Being a visual merchant is sort of like being a plastic surgeon."

Greenberg's clients include Bloomingdale's, Saks Fifth Avenue, and Louis Vuitton, to name a few. Greenberg also makes a regular appearance on HGTV's *Decorating Sense*.

Greenberg talks about getting a start in visual merchandising. "Usually when you start out in a big department store, they want you to choose a track, either hard goods or fashion." Hard goods include items such as pots and pans. "When you get really good at one track, then you can switch to the other. It's important to get experience on both sides."

Greenberg has a degree in fine art—painting, sculpting, and playing with clay—so being a visual merchant comes naturally. She says that formal education is not necessary to break into the field. "When I started out, half of the department came from housekeeping because they were always helping to move things around. You don't have to have an art department background. You need to love to work with your hands. Understand, however, that's it's not about your creativity alone; it's about your creativity and the store's point of view. Is it a Gap store or a department store? They are totally different.

"Being a visual merchant means making a story by coordinating the outfit with accessories such as handbags, shoes, and a belt. In cosmetics, you get to incorporate seasonal elements like leaves and pine cones for the fall. You must realize the theatrical aspect of what the store wants to represent."

Greenberg has a tip for those wanting to break into the field. "On September 1, go to every store you can, leave your resume with a photograph, and then call every two weeks. Retailers start to put up Christmas trees in September, and they need all the extra hands they can get. If you're good, they just might keep you after the holiday season is over."

According to Greenberg, visual merchandising can be physically demanding. "You work hard physically with long hours, and you have lots of deadlines. Before the store opens, you have to walk through your territory. Sometimes you're a glorified cleaning person. You have to go pick up everything that customers took out of place. People bought those pots and pans that were on your display yesterday, and you have to put all those pots and pans back, five days a week.

"If there is a sale going on, you may have to put the store's merchandise on different types of racks. If the manager decides to move the junior department from the fifth floor to the basement, you have to load everything up on racks and do it. And don't be surprised if after a week, they decide that they don't really like it there in the basement and now they want it moved to the second floor. You have to move the lettering, and if it's crooked, you move it again until it's straight. Sometimes there are surprise visits from

> regional headquarters, and everything has to be cleaned. You are not the ultimate boss."
>
> But Greenberg wouldn't trade it for the world. "The visual merchant gets to go into all of the stock rooms, and the whole store is our playground."

The Good News and Things to Consider

If you are creative and have an eye for color, decorating, staging, and lighting, then this may be the job for you. While visual merchandising can be glamorous, the job can be demanding physically. Visual merchants often have to climb ladders, move fixtures around, dress unwieldy mannequins, and the like. They also have to work evenings, weekends, and holidays, just like sales personnel.

So What Does a Visual Merchandiser Do?

A visual merchandiser spends time and energy making everything in the store look just right so that customers are more likely to make purchases. The visual merchandiser creates everything from window displays to center platforms and area ledges.

Visual merchandisers are creative, and have a solid knowledge of design principles, color, lighting, and staging. They also should have analytical abilities so that they can read company reports about what's selling and then create displays using that merchandise.

The visual merchandiser does not work alone. He or she must be able to take direction, and sometimes criticism, from management and buyers. The visual merchandiser is working as part of a team.

Employment Outlook

The United States Department of Labor forecasts that the demand for visual merchandisers will grow about as fast as the average growth of jobs in the United States through the year 2014. In the year 2004, 86,000 people were employed as visual merchandisers.

How Much Do Visual Merchandisers Earn?

As is the case for many other retail jobs, salaries vary greatly by geographic region. They tend to be higher in cities with higher costs of living. See Figure 3.3.

FIGURE 3.3: **MEDIAN SALARIES FOR VISUAL MERCHANDISERS**

	New York, NY	Los Angeles, CA	Dallas, TX
Visual Merchant	$ 49,845	$ 47,607	$ 43,010
Visual Merchant Director	$110,747	$105,774	$ 95,560

Source: Salary.com

Jobs Outside
the Store

As co-owner of The Comfortable Home furni-
ture store in a small mountain town in Colorado, Kathleen Johnson
performs nearly every duty in the store, including buying all the
merchandise that the store carries. Being a buyer is one of the more
glamorous jobs in retail, but it definitely takes quite a bit of skill.

Johnson tells how she and her husband got started in the furniture
business. "I've been in retail for a long time, but not in this field.

We started out together as antiques dealers and rented space on Broadway in Denver. We would go to auctions and fairs for merchandise. You always paid cash for it and hauled it away in a trailer. Buying was very simple. Then we noticed that the caliber of the merchandise started slipping a lot in antiques, and so we thought to incorporate new things, which was practically unheard of. We went to the Denver Merchandise Mart to look for those new things."

Once the Johnsons started buying new merchandise, they began expanding the markets they visited. "We went to Atlanta, and the following year we went to Dallas to check out their market. The antiques were still working for us, and then we started going to market in High Point, North Carolina, for new things."

Success brought rewards for the Johnsons, as well as an unexpected problem. "As we started becoming more and more successful, our landlord really gouged us on rent, and we made the move to Kittredge because we wanted to own our own building. We also moved our residence, because at the time, we were living outside of a town called Pine, and we had upsized to a 28-foot trailer. You cannot live in a subdivision with such a huge trailer."

Johnson discusses how being a good buyer means paying attention to your market. "The first year we moved to Kittredge, we were very different from how we are now. We had been successful with white furniture, the peely paint, cottagey look. It didn't even occur to us that these things would not be strong in this area.

"Then we went to the Roundtop market in Texas, and thought we should buy some European things. And they sold very well. We were listening to what people really wanted. My inventory has shifted so greatly, even in our small decor. Take a look at the architecture here: it's the European-country look, with high ceilings. It's rustic elegance, comfortable and easy to live with. People in this market have greater quantities of furniture, and we now have incredible sideboards and buffets. Those are pieces that really make a statement and work with the open architecture found in this area.

"This is a problem when we go to market, because so many pieces have a high sheen, and that doesn't work here. People here want something they can put their feet up on; this isn't Dallas or Atlanta, this is the Front Range.

"There are so many people who start out in antiques and want their stores to be a stamp of who they are, but you have to give people what they want. Go and see what's going on in your area.

"I know the majority of my customer base uses red, green, and gold, so I gear my upholstery items toward that. When I buy accessories for the store, I buy quite a bit of red, because that is what sells first.

> "Listening to your customer and getting into a field that you person-
> ally love—those are the ingredients to success."

■ ■ ■

In Chapter 3 we discussed retail jobs found in a store. In
this chapter, we're going to take a look at some of the retail
opportunities in a corporate headquarters setting. These positions include buyers, marketing associates, marketing research
associates, information systems managers, and accounting
and finance managers. For each of these jobs, we'll describe
the working environment, the qualifications, employment
outlook, and earnings.

Buyer

Retail buyers are responsible for purchasing the merchandise
to be sold in the store. A buyer may purchase goods locally, or
within the country, or even travel overseas.

The Good News and Things to Consider

If you are a recent college graduate, many of the larger department stores hire buyer assistants, sometimes called junior
buyers, who go into their training programs. Some firms do
promote from within, so if you are already working with a big
company and have received outstanding reviews, you may
have a chance at getting one of these plum positions. The U.S.

Department of Labor forecasts slower than average growth for this job. And, even though this is an office job, you can expect to put in extra hours on a seasonal basis or during big sales.

So What Does a Buyer Do?

Retail buyers buy all the goods for their stores. A buyer tries to get the best possible deal for his or her company in terms of price and quality. Their duties vary tremendously with the experience level of the buyer and the size of the company. When a buyer is first hired by a large company, he or she usually is put in charge of one small area and works up to an area of increased responsibility.

Laurel Humphrey, for example, started her retail career with Neiman Marcus in Dallas, Texas. She says, "I was accepted into their executive training program, and after a training period, I began as an assistant buyer. I started off buying stationery. I had two different buying experiences, and then went into buying designer jewelry, which included costume and semiprecious jewelry. None of the lines I was working with were overseas; everything came out of New York."

Buyers must study sales records and inventory levels of current stock, keep track of both foreign and domestic suppliers, and watch out for changes that may affect both the supply and demand of a product. One of the most important jobs a buyer has, in fact, is keeping track of new trends. Sometimes, a new trend is created virtually overnight. Demand may skyrocket for a new brand of boots mentioned on a national talk show, sending buyers scurrying to see how fast they can get those boots into their store for waiting customers.

Buyers are an integral part of the distribution and merchandising system. They closely follow the competition by reviewing advertising in the newspaper and other media. They track economic conditions to get a firm idea of how much inventory to order and how much consumers are willing to spend.

Buyers working for large companies may handle one area, while those working for smaller establishments may buy merchandise for the entire store. Small business owners often perform nearly all the duties in their stores, including the buying function.

Two factors have contributed to the increased responsibility for buyers in recent years. The first is the use of private-label merchandise, and the second is the consolidation of buying departments. Private-label merchandise is merchandise manufactured exclusively for one retailer. Buyers must ensure that the final product fits the standards of the retailer. Also, as large retailers merge with one another or simply seek to reduce overhead, buying departments are being downsized and consolidated. So there are fewer people doing the same amount of work.

When assistant buyers are promoted, they can begin to assist in planning and implementing sales promotion programs. Buying managers may work with other departments, including advertising, to create an advertising campaign. Together they will determine the best use of media, whether it be newspaper, direct mailings, television, or a combination of all three.

Buyers must stay in constant contact with store personnel to determine which products are selling well, which are not, and if there are requests from customers for certain merchandise that the store does not currently carry. Buyers also may work with visual merchandisers in the store to ensure that goods are properly displayed. Assistant buyers are often responsible for placing orders and checking on the status of orders.

Another critical job responsibility of buyers is determining the worthiness of suppliers and potential suppliers. In order to perform this function, buyers may attend trade shows and conferences, network with other professionals, and use the internet to glean any available information. More senior buyers usually visit potential suppliers to make certain they can indeed deliver. Because many firms have shortened the time frame on ordering and receiving merchandise, disruptions in the supply chain can be devastating for a business.

Some travel can be expected, especially in today's increasingly global economy. Therefore, it may be helpful for buyers to be familiar with other cultures and languages.

Working Conditions

Most buyers work in comfortable, climate-controlled offices. Buyers at all levels may work more than the 40-hour week because of special sales, conferences, or deadlines. It could be difficult to arrange for vacation during peak times.

Buyers, like most retail workers, need physical stamina to be able to endure the extra hours and the pressure, and sometimes, the travel. Buyers may have to travel within the United States to do business, or abroad.

Qualifications

Most retail companies prefer to hire candidates with a college degree, although some companies do not require it. Retailers prefer applicants with a bachelor's degree in business, or at least with a business emphasis. Regardless of whether or not the new hire has a degree, retailers are looking for candidates who are familiar with the merchandise they sell.

Even new hires with retail experience must learn the business practices of their new company. Training periods can last from one to five years. As junior buyers progress, many large retailers require them to work in the store for awhile so they can better understand that side of the business. Continuing education is increasingly important for buyers. Professional certification is increasingly sought after. Buyers must have outstanding communications skills as well as analytical skills. They should be fluent in the use of many computer software products as well as the internet. Buyers need to become adept in the art of negotiation and in supply-chain management.

Good candidates include those comfortable with reading and creating financial spreadsheets, as well as those who are good at planning and decision making. Junior buyers who wish to advance need to exhibit good leadership qualities, as they will eventually be expected to spend time supervising and mentoring future junior buyers, or sales associates should they move to the store side. As buyers advance, the top positions share the responsibility for overall planning and marketing with other top managers in the company. Continuing education is another important facet of being a buyer. Professional certification is becoming increasingly sought after.

Employment Outlook

According to the U.S. Department of Labor, the overall outlook for retail buyer jobs is expected to grow more slowly than average. Mergers and acquisitions in the retail industry have caused buying departments to consolidate in order to avoid duplication of efforts and to save money. Because these choice jobs are going to be a bit harder to come by, those with college educations should have an advantage.

Earnings

Keep in mind that higher level buyers earn more and that pay scales vary by location and size of the company. Buyers receive the same benefits package as other workers, including vacations, sick leave, life and health insurance, and pension plans, and may receive an employee discount.

The Bureau of Labor Statistics reports the following on earnings for buyers for May 2004:

Median Annual Earnings	$42,230
The lowest 10% earned less than	$24,380
The middle 50% earned between	$31,550–$57,010
The highest 10% earned more than	$79,340

Marketing

Marketing is a huge area of responsibility and the size of the marketing department varies greatly from company to company. The goal of marketing professionals is to figure out how best to meet the needs of their particular target market, and they do this by making decisions about what has traditionally been called the *4 Ps* of marketing. The *4 Ps* include product, price, place (distribution), and promotion. Marketing professionals may work with other departments in the company to make these decisions.

Under the concept of product, there is usually a department within the marketing area that works on product development, design, and quality assurance. Marketers also concern themselves with setting the appropriate prices for their products. The accounting area usually helps out with this function so that profit goals are met. Place refers to where and how the product is distributed. Many companies have their own in-house advertising departments that not only create advertising campaigns but also determine the best channels for advertising, be it television, newspaper, e-mail, radio, and some outlets.

Marketing researchers strive to provide accurate information regarding all these facets of the marketing mix. We're going to take a look at a general marketing job, and then we'll look at a specialized job within the marketing area.

The Good News and Things to Consider

Positions in the marketing area are expected to grow faster than the average growth rate for all jobs through 2014. Earnings are excellent, as would be expected because a college education is almost always a requirement for any job in a marketing department. The most common degree is a business degree with an emphasis in marketing.

So What Does a Marketing Professional Do?

The manager or director of the marketing department determines the goals of the department so that the company meets its overall goals in terms of market share and profitability. From these goals, the manager is then able to develop and execute marketing plans and programs. Programs can be short term and long term, and are always designed to ensure the profit growth and expansion of the company.

Marketing personnel also work with associates in the marketing research area so that the target market is firmly identified. This is done through research, analysis, and monitoring of financial, technological, and demographic factors. Marketing personnel are aware of new developments in the market and are prepared to capitalize on them. Marketing associates may also request that the marketing research department survey customers regarding new products.

If survey participants express sufficient interest in a potential new product, marketing associates then work with other departments in the company to develop that product. Sometimes the marketing department works with outside vendors on new product ventures as well.

Marketing personnel plan and supervise the company's advertising and promotion activities, including print, electronic, and direct-mail outlets. They may work with an inhouse advertising department or an outside advertising agency, which means working with artists and writers and overseeing copywriting, design, layout, and production of promotional materials.

Marketing personnel also monitor and review past activity through the use of marketing activity reports. Using this information, they may recommend changes for the future, such as pricing strategy or promotion so that the company realizes its goals in terms of profit, market share, and growth. Marketing personnel should know immediately if a particular product or advertising campaign isn't working and be prepared to alter strategies.

Working Conditions

Most marketing professionals work in pleasant office environments for 40-plus hours per week. Busy seasons vary from company to company.

What Are the Qualifications?

Most companies require a college degree to start out in the marketing department. Exceptions may be made for work experience. Obviously companies look for candidates with degrees in marketing, but they also are interested in graduates with liberal arts backgrounds, such as sociology and psychology. Many retail businesses prefer the manager or director of marketing have a graduate degree, but again, exceptions are made for those who demonstrate outstanding skills and have equivalent job experience.

Successful candidates will have outstanding communication skills, because marketing professionals are called upon to write reports for the company or articles for publication, give presentations to top management or the public, and interface with members of the business community. Outstanding analytical skills are also a necessity, because marketing professionals must create budgets, read reports regarding profitability, review statistical analyses from marketing research, and draw conclusions from sales reports.

Employment Outlook

The Bureau of Labor Statistics reports that college graduates with related experience, a high level of creativity, and strong communication skills have the best chances at getting one of the highly coveted jobs in marketing. It also reports that growth in this field is expected to be faster than the average for all occupations through the year 2014, due to increased competition.

Earnings

The Bureau of Labor Statistics reports that the median annual earnings for marketing managers was $87,640 in May 2004. According to a National Association of Colleges and Employers survey, starting salaries for marketing majors graduating in 2005 averaged $33,873. Salary levels for people in marketing vary substantially, depending on the size of the company, the location of the company, the experience of the candidate, education, and the level of responsibility of the position. Managers who work in the retail industry may get an employee discount as well as a yearly bonus.

Marketing Research

Marketing researchers provide information to marketers to help them make decisions regarding the best products to offer and the best possible ways to market those products.

The Good News and Things to Consider

Employment in this field is expected to grow faster than average, with a 20 percent growth rate predicted through the year 2014. Average pay for marketing research professionals is excellent, making it one of the higher paying jobs in retail. To work in marketing research, most companies require at least a bachelor's degree, and some companies require a master's degree. Continuing education is also imperative.

So What Does a Marketing Research Professional Do?

Marketing research professionals are somewhat like detectives, trying to find out all they can about what makes their customers tick. They can find out why a product wasn't successful, and what to do about it. Often marketing researchers can even predict whether or not a new product will be successful before money is poured into a product that will not sell. They snoop around and gather information on the competition.

Marketing researchers employ one of two methods to gather information. The first method involves finding information that has already been published, such as studies or statistics

PROFILE

Sue Stewart

Founder and President of Consumer Focus, Dallas, Texas

Information is vital to the success of marketing campaigns. Marketing managers need to know which products their customers want and at what prices. They also need information about the most effective way to advertise and distribute products. In order to get such information, marketing personnel turn to experts in marketing research.

Sue Stewart is the president and founder of Consumer Focus, a marketing research firm, as well as an author and sought-after speaker in the field. Stewart explains what first attracted her to market research when she was starting out. "I think it's like many things. I didn't know that was what I wanted, but when I was in school I really enjoyed the marketing research classes I took. I liked studying about the psychology of the consumer—what makes them make the choices that they make. I also thought it was interesting that the companies that are the most profitable find out what the consumer wants."

When Stewart finished her education, she began her career in a management training program. "I worked in a lot of different departments as part of the training program. I was lucky enough to find a position in the newly created marketing research department, and then I got to manage it very quickly."

So exactly how does someone do marketing research? Stewart explains, "Marketing research varies depending on the company and depending on what the current information needs are. The client may wish to know what their customers think about the client's product, their service, or even their advertising. You must work with the client to understand their information needs, and then figure out a way to get that information."

There are basically two ways to get the information. One is called secondary research: information that is already out there, waiting for the researcher to find it. "This secondary information could be information from the government or from a syndicated study, for example. If the information isn't already out there, then you must find it yourself by doing primary research. You either do quantitative or qualitative research.

"A common form of qualitative research is focus groups. With focus groups you gather small groups of people together to talk about the marketing information needed. You typically have 8 to 12 people in a group, and they have been specifically invited. They are in a room with a two-way mirror. The group sits on one side with a moderator, and the client sits on the other side of the mirror.

"The moderator has a general outline of the topics the group is going to discuss, and the moderator takes the group from a general subject to particular questions. People are asked to give their opinions. These results give ideas." But because the groups are small, the results cannot be projected back on the population. You simply get "Ah-ha!" information for the client.

The other type of primary research is quantitative, where surveys are conducted involving larger groups of people.

Stewart talks about the qualities good marketing research professionals share. "You should be an analytical person, be concerned about the underlying reasons for things, understand what the data means, and be able to interpret the data. It's important to be detail oriented. It's also good to have a marketing background. The more one knows about a particular industry, the more they can provide recommendations to relate back to the marketing question.

"It's best to have a degree; it helps you have more credibility with your clients. You should have a good basis in statistics. While there are packages that will run the statistical analysis for you, the background will help you in designing a questionnaire.

"Seasonality in marketing research is driven by the companies you work for. If they have seasonality, you will, too. Then there are the budget issues. People tend to have budgets for marketing research more toward the beginning of the fiscal year, or they may have money left over at the end of the year that they need to spend.

"Deadlines are extremely important. Everyone wants the data as quickly as possible.

"Travel depends more on the company you are working with more than anything else. If you are doing quite a number of focus groups, there can be travel associated with that, although you can also watch the groups from your home base.

"The internet has changed marketing research a bit, and companies can now do both qualitative and quantitative work online. About 20 percent of all focus groups are being done online. The biggest reason for this is that it saves money."

Stewart worked for many years for a Fortune 500 company in marketing research, and then in the marketing department before deciding to strike out on her own. "I thought about it for a couple of years before I left the company. I missed the marketing research work. I was very much a user of marketing research (in the marketing department) and I missed the detail work. I had the opportunity to open my own business when the company I worked for was sold."

compiled by the government. This method of information gathering is called secondary research.

The other method of getting questions answered is called primary research, and involves designing surveys or focus groups. Surveys may be sent through the mail, or conducted via telephone, internet, or even door-to-door. The questions on a survey must be phrased correctly, or the answers the participants give may be skewed. Marketing researchers must have a thorough knowledge of statistics as well in order to help determine how many people to include in a study so that the results are valid and meaningful and can be projected back on the population.

Focus groups are small groups of people, perhaps 8 to 12, who are selected from the broader target population. A moderator leads the group and questions them regarding their reactions to a particular product, advertising, or even pricing. The moderator is looking for opinions and emotional responses from the group. Results are qualitative, and because the groups are small, the results are not statistically significant.

After conducting the research, the market research analyst's job is to compile the data and present the findings to the client. Management then uses this data to modify the product, advertising, or pricing.

Working Conditions

Marketing research professionals spend some of their time with others, determining the needs of the client. They also spend time alone creating surveys, writing reports, researching, and evaluating statistical analysis. Often there are deadlines and tight schedules, which may require overtime. Marketing research professionals may travel to conduct research, including focus groups, and to conferences.

What Are the Qualifications?

Most companies require a bachelor's degree as a prerequisite for positions in marketing research. Other companies require a master's degree, especially for more technical positions. A strong analytical background with coursework in statistics is essential. Marketing researchers should also have completed courses in mathematics, psychology, sociology, business, and computer science. Communication skills are essential because marketing researchers must be able to communicate with the client to determine his or her needs. Excellent written and verbal skills also serve the analyst well when it comes time to write reports and to present findings to clients.

Employment Outlook

Prospects are outstanding for marketing researchers. According to the Bureau of Labor Statistics, market and survey researchers numbered 212,000 in 2004. Marketing research analysts aren't just employed in the retail industry but throughout the economy. Growth in employment of marketing researchers is forecast to be faster than the average for all occupations through 2014. One of the reasons demand should be strong is because as the economy becomes increasingly competitive, companies need to evaluate customer satisfaction and plan more effectively for the future.

Earnings

The Bureau of Labor Statistics reported the following figures for earnings for marketing researchers in May 2004:

Median annual earnings	$56,140
Lowest 10% less than	$30,890
Middle 50%	$40,510–$79,990
Highest 10%	$105, 870

Remember when looking at these figures that they include pay levels for entry positions, as well as for the more senior managers.

Computer and Information Systems Managers

In today's retail world, keeping up with the latest information systems technology is critical to staying competitive. Information systems managers plan, create, coordinate, and direct research in company's computer-related activities.

The Good News and Things to Consider

Employment for the information systems area is expected to grow faster than average for all occupations through the year 2014. Compensation for these positions is excellent. Systems managers work at least 40 hours per week but may have to work longer hours to meet deadlines or solve unexpected problems. Sometimes systems personnel are under intense pressure to create or modify systems within tight timeframes or budgets. Workers who sit in front of a computer for long periods of time often experience eyestrain, back pain, or hand and wrist problems such as carpal tunnel syndrome.

So What Does a Computer and Information Systems Manager Do?

Computer and information systems associates are vital to the success and profitability of retail companies. They oversee network security, direct internet operations, and design or select packaged inventory management systems. Proper inventory management means that merchandise is on the shelf ready for the customer to purchase, rather than sitting in a warehouse.

Another area under the domain of the information systems manager is that of electronic commerce. The internet offers the possibility of creating new relationships with customers. Integrating methods of distribution, or multichanneling, is one of the latest trends. The information systems manager works in conjunction with the marketing department to develop the electronic commerce system, or the information systems manager may work with an outside vendor to purchase a system, possibly customizing it.

Information systems personnel also plan and coordinate the installation and upgrading of hardware and software. They must stay current with the latest technology to make sure their company does not fall behind the competition.

INVENTORY MANAGEMENT

Al Slavin, a general store manager for a super Wal-Mart in San Antonio, Texas, talks about how his company's inventory management system works. "We're actually the leaders in the technology of point-of-sale, or perpetual inventory. We check merchandise off the truck in the back of the store, and it is entered into the system at that point. As the item is purchased by a customer, the system takes it out of the inventory, and the item gets re-ordered if necessary. I have 170,000 items in the store, and it's unbelievable how much it takes to manage that business. The system flows fairly well, but you have theft, which the system does not account for, and you have people who sometimes cut corners.

"We use a tool called Gemini, which looks like a laser gun out of *Star Trek.* You can use this to scan an item, and it will tell you how many you have sold of that item, how many you have left, how much the markup is, etc."

Finally, computer and information systems managers must maintain the security of their company's systems and protect their sites from hackers, viruses, and cyber terrorism. Cyber security is rapidly becoming a key issue facing most organizations, and this factor should in turn lead to even greater demand for competent managers.

Working Conditions

Computer and information systems managers work in offices, usually from Monday through Friday. Some positions call for weekend work, for instance, for those manning help desks. If a system goes down or a new system is being installed, upgraded, or developed, overtime may be necessary.

What Are the Qualifications?

Most companies require at least a bachelor's degree for management positions, although many prefer a graduate degree such as an MBA with technology as the core component. This MBA differs from a traditional MBA in that there is heavy emphasis on information technology. Because of the increased importance of technology in businesses, information managers are making not only important technology decisions for their companies but also important business decisions.

Information managers should have outstanding communications skills because they need to thoroughly understand the wants and needs of those using the systems. They should also be able to explain highly technical work in nontechnical terms to individuals outside their department.

Employment Outlook

According to the Bureau of Labor Statistics, employment of computer and information systems managers is expected to grow faster than the average for all occupations through the year 2014. As technology advances, so will the demand for computer-related workers.

Earnings

According to the Bureau of Labor Statistics, earnings for professionals in the computer and information systems area vary by specialty and level of responsibility. Median annual earnings in May 2004 were $92,570. The middle 50 percent earned between $71,650 and $118,330.

According to Robert Half International, a professional staffing and consulting services firm, average starting salaries in 2005 for high level information technology managers ranged from $80,250 to $112,250. According to a 2005 survey by the National Association of Colleges and Employers, starting salary offers for those with an MBA, a technical undergraduate degree, and 1 year or less of experience averaged $52,300; for those with a master's degree in management information systems/business data processing, the starting salary averaged $56,909. Computer and information systems managers working in the retail industry may also receive employee discounts on merchandise purchased from their employers as well as bonuses.

Accounting and Finance Managers

Accountants and financial managers who work for retail firms make certain that important financial records are kept, taxes are paid properly and on a timely basis, and accounts are collected and creditors paid. If the company is a publicly owned institution, financial managers ensure that funds are handled wisely so that shareholders realize the full potential of their investments.

The Good News and Things to Consider

Opportunities in this field are outstanding, as changing financial regulations, an increase in the number of businesses, and greater scrutiny of company finances drive growth. Most of the positions in this field require a bachelor's degree in accounting or finance. Some positions require a master's degree or a professional accreditation such as the Certified Public Accountant designation.

So What Does an Accounting or Financial Manager Do?

Management accountants are also called cost or corporate accountants, and they record and analyze the financial information of the companies for which they work. They are concerned with budgeting, performance evaluation, cost management, and asset management. Management accountants may also be involved in strategic planning or development of new products. They prepare reports for groups within the company, as well as for groups outside the company, including stockholders, the Internal Revenue Service, creditors, and regulatory agencies.

Internal auditors ensure that their organization is not mismanaging funds or committing fraud. Internal auditing is becoming increasingly important. There are many types of specialized auditors, including electronic data processing, legal, bank, and insurance auditors.

Most financial managers work extensively with computers and special software packages that help them do their jobs.

Working Conditions

Financial and accounting managers work at least a standard 40-hour-per-week schedule, Monday through Friday. They may work periods of overtime during busy seasons, such as during the annual budgeting process or during tax season.

What Are the Qualifications?

The majority of positions in this field require at least a bachelor's degree in accounting or finance. Some companies prefer candidates to have a master's degree in business administration with a concentration in accounting or finance. They may require that certain positions be filled with accountants who are Certified Public Accountants.

Financial professionals should not only have an aptitude for facts and figures but also have good written and oral communications skills, as well as computer skills. Probably one of the most important assets a candidate should have is that of integrity.

Employment Outlook

The Bureau of Labor Statistics reports that accountants and auditors held about 1.2 million jobs in 2004 and that growth in the number of these positions is going to be greater than the average growth for all occupations. A number of factors are contributing to this growth: changing financial laws and regulations, the need to replace those who retire or transfer to other occupations, and an increased scrutiny of company finances.

Earnings

Median annual wage and salary earnings of accountants and auditors were $50,770 in May 2004, according to the Bureau of Labor Statistics. The middle half of the occupation earned between $39,890 and $66,900. The top 10 percent of accountants and auditors earned more than $88,610, and the bottom 10 percent earned less than $32,320.

According to a salary survey conducted by the National Association of Colleges and Employers, bachelor's degree candidates in accounting received starting offers averaging $43,269 a year in 2005; master's degree candidates in accounting were offered $46,251 initially.

Real Estate and Store Development Manager

The store itself speaks to the customers as strongly as any salesperson. Businesses must be prepared to respond immediately and effectively to customers' changing wants and desires. Are customers now shopping in a new suburban mall that threatens to take away business from existing store locations? Is the store currently located in a shopping area that has become shabby and unsafe? Is an urban area that is being completely renovated an appropriate location for a new store? How many new stores should be opened this year across the country?

These are just a sampling of the questions that the store development manager or vice president deals with every day. This manager is the person who helps the company find sites for new stores, plans remodeling of old stores, and manages the real estate portfolio for large companies.

So What Does a Store Development Manager Do?

Store development managers are responsible for planning all of the store development activities, including locating possible sites for new stores, managing current real estate portfolios, lease management, construction management, and store maintenance management. In addition to opening new stores, the store development manager coordinates the remodeling of older stores and the closing of stores that are not profitable.

The store development manager commissions market research and analysis on current trends so as to recommend strategic changes. This manager also works closely with other departments such as accounting and finance to review the real estate portfolio to maximize profitability and to develop models to be used for strategic planning. The store development manager also teams up with the marketing department to develop or change store prototypes.

Store development professionals are experts in real estate matters and can advise on negotiations, strategy, corporate policy, and preferred lease language. They also coordinate with the inhouse legal department in these matters. The store development manager also manages relationships with landlords and developers.

When a new store is opened or remodeled, the store development manager stays on top of every aspect of the process, ensuring that everything is done as promised by personnel within the company and by any outsourced third-party professionals. The store development manager manages relationship with vendors as well.

Store development managers are on the watch for any new real estate opportunities and make recommendations to management based on these new developments. They oversee negotiations for the renewal of leases, making certain that the company gets the best possible deal. They are also involved in the budgeting process and concerned with keeping expenses in line, resources, and financial projections.

Working Conditions

The real estate and store development manager may have to travel 30–40 percent of the time. The rest of the time may be spent at the home office.

What Are the Qualifications?

Though the requirements differ from company to company, most organizations require that candidates for employment have a college degree. The area of preferred study changes, depending on the position. For example, for those store development positions that are responsible for the construction of new stores, a degree in construction management or architecture is required. For positions that are responsible for the actual design of new stores, a degree in interior design or architecture may be the prerequisite.

Start Your Retail Career

FIGURE **4.1: MEDIAN SALARIES FOR EXPERIENCED STORE DEVELOPMENT ASSOCIATES**

Store Development Positions	New York, NY	Los Angeles, CA	Dallas, TX
Retail Store Planning and Construction Director	$125,616	$119,976	$108,390
Executive	$143,382	$136,944	$123,719

Source: Salary.com

All candidates should have solid financial and analytical skills. Strong negotiating and influencing skills will serve the manager who will be working with mall developers or other landlords. Finally, outstanding communication and people skills are a must, as most store developers need to coordinate with a wide variety of in-store people and third-party individuals.

Earnings

Starting salaries for a position in the store development area are in line with other professional positions, at around $35,000 per year. But the salary levels for this position vary substantially, depending on the size of the company, the location of the company, the experience level of the candidate, education, and the level of responsibility of the position. See Figure 4.1 for some sample salaries. Managers who work in the retail industry may also get an employee discount as well as a yearly bonus.

The Working
Environment

PROFILE

Micheal Klein

William Noble Rare Jewels

Dallas, Texas

It's an extraordinary world, the world of rare jewels, featuring one-of-a-kind gems created millions of years ago under conditions of extreme heat and pressure. William Noble Rare Jewels is an upscale boutique that emphasizes such treasures, as well as designer, estate, and antique jewelry. The firm claims to have sold some of the rarest and most valuable pieces of jewelry in the world and boasts of having the largest new and estate inventory in the Southwest.

It takes a unique individual to work in such an environment. Micheal Klein, salesman extraordinaire, thrives in this world, where each salesperson must have at least 20 years of experience before even being considered for a position with the team.

Klein first became interested in the jewelry business after a terrible personal tragedy. "My father was a pharmacist in Detroit, and he owned a drugstore/liquor store. He was murdered in a hold-up. The plan had been for me to become a pharmacist and work with him. I worked there for a year after he was gone, but I just didn't want to be a pharmacist any longer.

"So I called up a jeweler in Detroit, and worked there for six months. I saw all those little festive things going out in little boxes, and I became a firm believer in the 'Good things come in little packages' philosophy. In 1980, I moved from Detroit to Dallas. I had nothing, and I lived with a relative. My goal was to work for a prestigious jeweler. I interviewed with Linz Brothers and worked there for four years.

"I was then hired away by Fred Joaillier, the international French jeweler. That was a wonderful job. Working for an international firm taught me how to be an international thinker and mover. You'll notice on the web site [of William Noble Rare Jewels] that I spell it 'jeweller,' the way they do in Europe. I am not European, but I see high-end, well-heeled customers, and they are used to being in the House of Chanel or the House of Fred. When I spell it 'jewellry,' while some people may think I do not know how to spell, others will think 'This guy knows what he is talking about.'"

After 6 years, Klein moved to Neiman Marcus in the precious jewels department, and worked there for 14 years. He joined the William Noble team in 2003.

Klein emphasizes that everything in this business is about perception. "I am self-trained, and self-taught, with years of experience. I do not sell paper. I sell romance, love, and quality, and that's what people buy when they buy jewelry. If you want to buy a piece of jewelry as an investment, please go see Smith Barney instead. The ring you buy from me will give you a lot of pleasure over the years; it's never sold as an investment.

"If you don't like what you are doing, do something else. You've got to believe in what you are doing. I'll apologize for price once, but I'll never apologize for quality. I never want to apologize because something is inferior. Quality lasts forever. It's easier to sell for me because I believe in the product. If you are trying to sell something you don't believe in, it doesn't work. I love my job. I love my life.

"I never see the zeroes on any price. I treat the sale and the merchandise the same whether it's $500, or $5,000, or $500,000. The zeroes make a difference to the customer, but not to me. I'm not intimidated by the zeroes. Without question, I give the same level of service regardless of the numbers."

Klein is the consummate salesman, finding ways to make even the wildest dreams come true for his clients. "I recently sold a dog collar for a six-and-one-half-pound dog. There were three stones in it totaling 40 carats, with a platinum buckle and tongue for a cost of over a million dollars. I am currently working on another collar for the same client, who now has a second dog. This one started out with a 14-carat stone center. I did go and measure the dog's neck.

"I've never put a piece of jewelry in a box for a customer who wasn't happy. Every time they leave, they are happy. And when the recipient gets it, I know they are going to be happy, and if they are not, I am going to get the ability to make them happy. So one way or another, I am getting to deal with happy people. It's a sparkling, fun, exciting business. And I get to hold things that Mother Nature makes that are rare. This is a Mother Nature business. It's real, and it's not plastic. There's a limited supply.

"It's a wonderful environment. I wear beautiful suits to work, with French cuffs, and work in an elegant, refined, and sophisticated industry. I'm happy every day."

■ ■ ■

Now that we've taken a look at the various types of jobs available inside retail stores and at corporate headquarters in Chapters 3 and 4, let's take a look at some of the environments in which retailers work. When most people think about retail, the first businesses that usually come to mind are clothing or department stores, which do make up a large part of the retail industry. And yet automobile dealers and grocery stores are also retail establishments, and make up a huge portion of the retail industry in terms of sales, number of establishments, and number of employees. These subsectors of retail are so important that the United States Bureau of Labor Statistics sometimes looks at the retail industry as part of the trade industry, with the following categories:

- Automobile dealers
- Clothing, accessory, and general merchandise stores
- Grocery stores
- Wholesale trade

We will be taking a look at the first three categories and some of their subcategories.

The Clothing, Accessory, and General Merchandise Sector

This is a huge category in the retail industry, made up of department stores, supercenters, warehouse club stores, dollar stores, boutiques, large format stores, category killers, and general merchandise stores.

The Good News and Things to Consider

Many of the jobs in this sector do not require a college degree. Many people get their first job in this industry because there is no formal education requirement. There are many part-time jobs available; nearly one quarter of the sales work force in this industry is working part time. Earnings, however, are relatively low for many of the positions in this industry.

The Environment

As the name implies, department stores are arranged by departments, and no one line of merchandise dominates. Each department is headed by a manager. Department stores usually carry linens, cosmetics, costume and fine jewelry, shoes, clothing for men, clothing for women and children, appliances, electronics, kitchen items and china, and perhaps furniture. Department stores sometimes offer services such as photography or travel help. Discount department stores have fewer employees available for customer service and have centrally located cashiers, while more upscale stores offer greater customer service and personal service features such as tailoring.

Warehouse club stores and supercenters are the fastest growing segment of this sector and feature low prices as one of the draws. Items are often sold in bulk. These warehouses usually require consumers to purchase a yearly membership in order to shop there. They offer little in the way of customer service.

Clothing and accessory stores may sell one line of items, such as shoes, handbags and belts, perfume, lingerie, or even tuxedos. The staff in these smaller stores tends to be quite

THE BOUTIQUE CUSTOMER

Micheal Klein, of William Noble Rare Jewels, discusses how the boutique customer is very different from other retail customers. "Always remember that your client is above you, and that you are beneath the client. Never put yourself on the same level as the client. You have to let them believe that they are better traveled than you, they wear better jewelry, because they want to be the top dog. I drove a Volkswagen for 18 years. It was nice and it was always clean. I needed the sale. I wasn't the fat cat. I always dressed well, had a manicure, but I was never on the same level. Don't match wits with them. It's all perception."

knowledgeable and can offer excellent customer service. Many of these stores are located in shopping malls across the country.

Boutique retailing can be thought of as the opposite of the large format store. Boutiques do not strive to provide "one-stop shopping," nor do they cater to all people. Instead, boutiques strive to serve a narrow niche in the marketplace to satisfy the needs of a limited number of people. Boutiques stock exclusive and often unique, one-of-a-kind merchandise. Most boutiques carry jewelry, gifts, designer clothing, and the like. If the boutique carries clothing, it is often narrowed down to a specialized segment of the market, such as children's upscale clothing or lady's evening wear.

Customers who purchase boutique items want an item that defines them as a person. The customer may want to stand out in the crowd by being the owner of something exclusive that tells the world that the customer has a sense of fashion or good taste, or has reached the pinnacle of success.

Extremely personalized customer service is another feature that distinguishes boutiques from other retailers. If the boutique does not have what the customer wants, often they will special order the merchandise or have it created, as in the case of upscale jewelry stores.

The boutique itself differs greatly from other establishments. Customers get a certain "feeling" when they shop at a boutique, because a certain atmosphere pervades. This atmosphere strikes a chord with the customer, enticing him or her to buy. A boutique specializing in unique, upscale clothing may be lavishly decorated, with chandeliers, leather furniture, and specialized lighting. Instead of metal fixtures, antique furniture may serve to display the merchandise. Or in the case of boutiques catering to children, there might be train sets overhead, huge stuffed animals, or child-sized furniture to draw even the smallest of shoppers inside.

Working Conditions

To work in the clothing, accessory, and general merchandise industry, employees need to have good physical stamina and should be willing to work nights, weekends, and some holidays. Remember that for most establishments in this sector, the Christmas holidays are the busiest time of the year, and as a result, usually no one can take vacation during the last quarter of the year.

Employment Outlook

The clothing, accessory, and general merchandise subsector of the retail industry is enormous, with nearly 27 percent of all retail employees working in this segment. Department stores accounted for most of the jobs, but only about 7 percent of the number of establishments. Another characteristic of this subsector is that employment is found across the country, from large urban areas to small towns; so even if you live in a smaller city, there should be opportunity.

Workers tend to be young in this industry, with 31 percent under the age of 24 in 2004, compared with 14 percent for all industries. More than one quarter of workers are employed part time.

The Outlook

According to the Bureau of Labor Statistics, the growth rate for the clothing, accessory, and general merchandise subsector of retail is expected to be about 10 percent, compared with an overall growth rate of 14 percent for all industries. Job openings will be plentiful for first-time job seekers and people seeking part-time employment because of high turnover.

One of the reasons for the slower growth here is the expected limited growth in clothing and accessory stores, as discount department stores and supercenters take market share; the latter two types of businesses are less labor intensive.

Internet shopping will shift opportunities from traditional retail occupations to new occupations, such as internet sales managers, webmasters, technical support personnel, and other related workers. New developments in technology will also affect employment. As automated re-ordering systems become more common, the need for buyers may be reduced.

Earnings

One of the reasons that earnings for nonsupervisory workers in the clothing, accessory, and general merchandise stores are well below the average for all workers in the private industry is because there is a high proportion of part-time and less experienced workers.

See Figure 5.1 for the average weekly and hourly wages for the clothing, accessory, and general merchandise sector.

Grocery Stores

Grocery stores are everywhere, and most of us shop at one at least once a week. Grocery stores sell a wide variety of fresh produce and meats, and preserved foods as well. Most of the items sold in a grocery are for customers to take home and prepare meals for consumption at home. Stores range in size from mom-and-pop stores to megastores that carry more than just grocery items to convenience stores where people often buy fuel. Grocery stores represent a huge segment of the retail industry, employing just under 20 percent of all retail workers.

FIGURE 5.1: **AVERAGE EARNINGS OF NONSUPERVISORY WORKERS: 2004**

Industry Segment	Weekly	Hourly
Total, private industry	$529	$15.67
Total, general merchandise stores	301	10.32
Warehouse clubs and supercenters	328	9.94
Other general merchandise stores	317	9.93
Discount department stores	307	9.93
Department stores	290	10.67
Total, clothing and clothing accessory stores	268	10.55
Men's clothing stores	376	13.06
Family clothing stores	237	9.57
Shoe stores	241	9.46
Women's clothing stores	236	11.19

Source: United States Bureau of Labor Statistics, 2004.

The Good News and Things to Consider

There will be many job openings in the grocery store sector because of the high turnover rate and because of the size of the industry. Management positions are usually filled by college graduates, so to get ahead in this sector, a college education is a great idea. All workers in the store need to be in excellent physical condition.

What Is the Environment Like in the Grocery Store Industry?

Next time you go shopping in a grocery store, take a look around at the workers. You will notice that many of them are young. As a matter of fact, nearly one third of all workers in the grocery store sector are people ages 16–24. This is because many of the jobs in the store, such as baggers, do not require any formal education, training, or previous experience.

Grocery stores provided 2.4 million wage and salary jobs in 2004, making them one of the largest industries. Nearly 31 percent of all grocery store employees worked part time, and the average workweek of nonsupervisory workers was 30.8 hours.

The Bureau of Labor Statistics reports that most grocery stores are small, employing fewer than 50 workers. And yet most of the jobs are found in the largest stores, with 74 percent of the workers employed in establishments with more than 50 workers.

The traditional inner city store that carries a limited selection of goods has been giving way to the larger supercenter for quite some time. These supercenters not only are predominant in the suburban areas but also are being built in urban areas. Supermarkets not only carry a wide variety of foods, but also carry dry goods and often include specialty departments such as seafood stores, bakeries, delicatessens, pharmacies, and floral departments.

Some of the largest supermarkets may even offer automotive services, basic banking, on-site film processing, and optical services. At the other end of the spectrum, convenience stores sell a limited range of grocery items along with fuel. Convenience stores may also provide automatic teller machines, money orders, and some food for immediate consumption.

An interesting fact about the grocery store environment is that over 22 percent of all employees in the stores belong to a union, compared with 14 percent for all industries. Employees who work in chain stores are more likely to belong to a union or be covered by a contract than workers in independent grocery stores.

The management of grocery stores has become increasingly complex and technical. Managers of large stores are responsible for millions of dollars and hundreds of employees, and must use sophisticated software to manage budgets, schedule work, track and order goods, manage shelf space, and assess product profitability.

Cashiers make up the largest occupation in grocery stores, accounting for 34 percent of all workers. Stock clerks, who stock shelves, account for another 15 percent. There are also butchers, poultry, fish, and meat processors, clerical workers, bakers, chefs, food preparation workers, demonstrators and product promoters, freight and stock movers, cleaning workers, first-line managers, purchasing managers, and general and operations managers. In large stores, there may also be marketing and sales managers, pharmacists, florists, and inspectors.

Large Format Stores

Large format stores are those where shopping truly is one-stop. Customers can purchase groceries as well as an array of other products ordinarily found in drug stores, or even department stores. In recent studies, consumers in many developing retail markets around the world express their preference for large formats. Shoppers say they enjoy the convenience of one-stop shopping. For now, traditional supermarkets are the mainstay of the weekly shopping, but large format stores are continuing to increase in popularity.

Working Conditions

Grocery stores are generally pleasant places to work, with clean, well-lit, and climate-controlled areas. Sometimes dealing with the public can be difficult. Most grocery stores are open quite a few hours, and some even operate 24 hours a day. Workers are needed to cover all these hours. These extended hours are often appealing to students or to employees who have another job.

What Are the Qualifications?

The majority of positions in a grocery store do not require formal training or a college education. Cashiers are trained for a few days before getting out on the floor, while butchers and bakers may learn their trade at a vocational school. Candidates who are interested in management positions generally have a college degree. Programs are available at the junior and community college levels as well as at universities in food management, food marketing, and supermarket management. Other business degrees are also acceptable.

Employment Outlook

Although the Bureau of Labor Statistics projects a growth rate of only 7 percent in jobs in the grocery store sector, compared with 14 percent for all industries, there still should be plenty of opportunities for employment because the industry is so large and turnover is high. Unlike other retail areas like the automobile dealer sector, grocery stores are not as affected by swings in the economy. After all, we all need to eat.

Earnings

The Bureau of Labor Statistics reports that earnings in the grocery store industry are considerably lower than the average for all industries because there are a large number of entry-level and part-time positions. Full-time workers often receive the usual benefits: health and life insurance, paid vacations, and sick leave.

Managers make a salary, and oftentimes, a bonus based on the department or store performance. See Figure 5.2 for a breakdown of pay by area.

Automotive Dealers

The motor vehicle and parts dealers industry is an important subsector of the retail industry. Sales of over $800 million in the year 2002 accounted for just over one quarter of all retail sales for the year.

The Good News and Things to Consider

Most dealerships do not require college educations for the sales staff, and earnings in this industry are relatively high compared with other retail industries. On the other hand, employees of automobile dealers often work more than 40 hours per week, and because automobile dealers are open evenings and weekends, employees must cover those hours. Automobile sales are strongly affected by cycles in the economy. When times are good, people splurge and buy a new car. When times are bad, they make do with the car they already own.

What Is the Environment Like in the Automobile Dealer Industry?

Automobile dealers are the bridge between automobile manufacturers and the consumer. New car sales account for the vast majority of sales in the industry, and new car dealers employ nine out of ten workers; used car dealers employ the remaining

FIGURE 5.2: MEDIAN HOURLY EARNINGS IN GROCERY STORES: 2004

Occupation	Grocery Stores	All Industries
First-line supervisors/managers of retail sales workers	$15.08	$15.73
Butchers and meat cutters	13.00	12.45
Retail salespeople	9.24	8.98
Stock clerks and order fillers	8.94	9.66
Customer service representatives	8.69	12.99
Combined food preparation and serving workers, including fast food	8.59	7.06
Food preparation workers	8.54	8.03
Laborers and freight, stock, and material movers, hand	8.25	9.67
Cashiers	7.90	7.81
Packers and packagers, hand	7.07	8.25

Source: United States Bureau of Labor Statistics, 2004.

one out of ten workers. Once the new car is sold to a customer, that customer often returns for servicing, parts, and repairs for the time the customer owns the car. Many dealers offer not only cars but financing as well, creating a one-stop shopping experience for buyers.

The sale of new cars is not only affected by turns in the economy but also by interest rates. When interest rates are high, car dealers must offer greater incentives to customers to motivate them to purchase. People's decisions to buy cars are also influenced by the popularity of particular models the manufacturer offers and the intensity of competition with other dealers.

Many automobile dealers have an aftermarket sales department. This department sells service contracts and insurance to buyers. They may also offer extended warranties and additional services such as undercoat sealant and environmental paint protection packages.

Technology is changing the automobile dealer industry in several ways. The first involves the quality of today's new cars. Due to improvements in technology, cars are more durable, which in turn has led to more high-quality used cars being available. There is now a strong market for certified, pre-owned cars, enabling customers who cannot afford the price of a new luxury car to still get a slightly used version of the make and model of the car they desire. When the economy takes a downturn, the market for used cars improves.

Another way technology is changing the industry is through the use of the internet. Dealers are using the internet to sell new and used cars. Because customers can access vehicle reviews and compare different makes, models, features, and prices, customers are much better informed about their choices. As a result, salespeople may spend less time informing customers of a particular car's features.

A final trend in this industry involves the move toward consolidation. Smaller dealerships are giving way to larger establishments, which can typically offer customers lower prices and more services. Automobile dealers have an average of 25 employees per establishment, compared with an average of 14 employees per establishment among all retail businesses.

Working Conditions

Because dealers are open days, evenings, and weekends, employees must work these hours to provide coverage. According to the Bureau of Labor Statistics, 84 percent of automobile dealer employees worked full time in 2004, and more than a third of these workers worked more than 40 hours per week. Note that there are fewer part-time employees in this sector than in the grocery industry or the clothing and general merchandise industry.

Some people find the competitive nature of selling difficult. Most companies issue sales quotas, and if they are not met, corrective action, including dismissal, is taken. Because of the stressful nature of the job, turnover can be high.

Employment Outlook

The automobile dealer industry provided about 1.3 million wage and salary jobs in 2004. Sales, installation, maintenance, and repair workers accounted for 63 percent of the employees, while management, office and administrative support, and transportation and material moving made up another 35 percent.

The Bureau of Labor Statistics projects that growth in employment in the automobile dealer industry will increase by 12 percent over the period from 2004 to 2014, less than the 14 percent growth rate for all industries combined. Remember that the automobile industry is strongly affected by consumer confidence and the economy.

As the population grows in the United States, so does demand for automobiles. Competition for managerial jobs will remain keen.

Jobs in the Automobile Dealer Industry

Chapter 3 already talked about the retail salesperson job in depth. Like other retail businesses, the salesperson can make or break the business. Sales representatives account for 36 percent of the auto dealer industry employment. One of the differences between auto dealer sales representatives and other retail industry sales representatives is that in the automobile dealer industry, salespeople must be extremely knowledgeable about the features and options available. The salesperson usually gains this expertise through special training. Like all salespeople, those working in the automobile dealer industry must be well groomed and tactful, and have outstanding people skills. Because automobile purchases are significant for customers in terms of financial commitment, customers want to buy a car from someone they respect and trust.

Managers of sales associates are most often promoted from the ranks. These managers hire and train the sales force and are the lead negotiators between the salespeople and the

FIGURE **5.3:** **MEDIAN HOURLY EARNINGS FOR AUTOMOBILE DEALER POSITIONS: 2004**

Occupation	Automobile Dealers	All Industries
First-line supervisors/managers of retail sales workers	$31.80	$15.73
First-line supervisors/managers of mechanics, installers, and repairers	25.22	24.20
Retail salespeople	18.61	8.98
Automotive service technicians and mechanics	18.30	15.60
Counter and rental clerks	17.87	8.79
Automotive body and related repairers	17.73	16.68
Parts salespeople	15.16	12.32
Bookkeeping, accounting, and auditing clerks	12.93	13.74
Office clerks, general	10.55	10.95
Cleaners of vehicles and equipment	8.98	8.41

Source: United States Bureau of Labor Statistics, 2004.

customers. Other jobs include repair technicians, service advisors and managers, parts salespeople and managers, office and administrative workers, and general and operations managers who are ultimately in charge of the entire business.

What Are the Qualifications?

Many jobs in the automobile dealer industry do not require a college education, although each dealership has its own requirements. As with other jobs in the retail industry, although a college education is certainly not a prerequisite for a sales job, most companies prefer candidates for management positions to have a college degree. Technicians obviously require vocational training in all aspects of automobile care.

Earnings

The Bureau of Labor Statistics reports that the average weekly earnings of nonsupervisory workers were $634 in 2004, which was substantially higher than the average $371 per week for the retail trade. Most salespeople are paid a commission on sales. The dealer's geographic location and size are also factors in pay scales. Figure 5.3 gives median hourly wages for various jobs in this sector.

Try Before
You Buy

PROFILE

Lily Kender

University of Florida, Gainesville

Intern at PetSmart

An internship is the perfect way to discover if a chosen career is right for you, or in Lily Kender's case, to uncover a career in an industry she had not previously considered. Kender, a senior at the University of Florida in Gainesville, discusses how an internship changed her future. "I always knew I wanted to go into business, and my first major was accounting. But then I decided to major in economics because I liked the broader view in the business world. I am also getting a minor in entrepreneurship, which is a relatively new area they have been introducing around the country. It involves creating new ideas, leadership, and opening up your mind to new businesses."

During her early college years, Kender's plan was to get a job at the corporate headquarters of a company after graduation. "The atmosphere with most of my friends and the clubs I was in seemed to stress getting a high-end job at a corporation. No one was ever talking about working in a store. I wasn't even considering retail because I thought it was sort of a dead end, and not much money in it unless you owned your own company."

Cecilia Schulz, the associate director at the Center for Retailing Education and Research at the University of Florida, convinced Kender otherwise. "Cecilia Schulz was telling me that I should consider the retailing internships because there were great opportunities within stores, and that a lot of people actually do want to stay at the store level.

"There were a lot of different companies participating in the program, traditional companies like JCPenney. But I picked PetSmart in Ocoee, Florida, because I love business and I love animals, and I thought it would be a great combination. I found that PetSmart is a very innovative company, and they are above retail standards in customer service. In training, they really focus on meeting the customer's needs. They teach you to be a pet detective of sorts and find out what the customer really needs, like pet training, for example.

"In the beginning I shadowed the manager, and then there were workbooks. The workbooks really helped out so that the manager didn't have to spend all the time training. I learned a lot through experience, such as the opening and closing techniques, payroll, and scheduling. There's actually a lot more to it than I thought. I didn't realize the amount of work that goes into being a manager. I didn't know if it would be rewarding, but it was when I saw customers being satisfied.

"My internship started off my retail education. The internship itself lasted ten weeks, and during that time I was also taking retail math. I worked full time, 45 hours, as all managers are required to work that many hours. I also went to a symposium featuring different companies."

Kender is not exactly sure where she'll work when she graduates, but she definitely is thinking about a career with PetSmart. "I also enjoy fashion, so perhaps a career in a department store is also an option. I'd like to start off as a manager, and then I'd like to work my way into the corporate level so that I'll be the most knowledgeable.

I was reluctant to do this, but then I got the motivation. I would advise people to give it a try. You might find you like it. The most rewarding part of all is helping out a customer."

■ ■ ■

In this chapter we'll discuss the benefits of a college internship as well as list some of the companies offering internships. We'll also discuss why you might consider working part-time, and what the pros and cons are of doing so.

Internships

College internships are one of the most exciting ways to give the retail industry a try before you decide if it's for you. Even if you already know retail is for you, an internship may give you an opportunity to gain experience in an area you had not previously considered. Although each university has its own rules about internship programs, there are some basics that are consistent across most programs.

The Basics

Internships are completed for course credit, so the student gains not only crucial experience in the industry but also credit toward graduation. During the internship, students must keep in close contact with the university through a series of assignments to ensure that both the students and the retailers are getting all they can out of the experience.

Retail companies may have their own list of qualifications for interns. Many require that the student be either a junior or senior and have a minimum grade point average of 3.0 or higher. Potential candidates for internships should demonstrate a strong interest in the retail industry as well as leadership qualities.

Internships are generally served during the summer vacation, and last for eight to ten weeks. Some companies have longer programs that extend to eight months.

Many times interns are paid a salary as they are exposed to a variety of retail experiences. The intern may be placed in the store, in the buying office, or even in corporate headquarters. Internship positions are often available in the following areas, depending on the company:

Advertising
Buying
Corporate communications
Design or merchandise coordinating
Employee services
Facilities
Financial services
Information services
Internet
Inventory management

Product development
Quality assurance
Sales

The Benefits

Internships are a win-win opportunity for everyone. Retailers benefit from internships because they get the opportunity to assess the intern's potential for a career in their firm. According to a report published by the National Association of Colleges and Employers (NACE), employers will have even more internship opportunities for college students in the future. Employers reported that they plan to increase the number of internships by almost 10 percent. In this study, more than 75 percent of the businesses said that the main purpose of their programs is to feed their college hiring programs. On average, businesses were able to convert 53 percent of their interns into full-time employees.

Potential new hires with solid experience in the field are so valuable to employers that in many instances the starting salary is higher when they are offered full-time jobs, according to the NACE. Almost half (46.2 percent) of the employers report that they offer higher starting salaries to those candidates who have internship experience. Some employers add a set percentage on top of the entry-level salary or they review the candidate's experience and determine increases on a case-by-case basis.

Obviously internship programs are affected by the economy. Downturns in the economy often result in scaling back of new hires, which in turn results in scaling back internship programs.

**A SAMPLE OF COMPANIES
OFFERING INTERNSHIP PROGRAMS**

Here are just a few of the retail companies offering internships to college students:

Abercrombie and Fitch	The Limited Brands
Atlanta Apparel Mart	L.L. Bean
Beall's	Macy's
Body Shop	Neiman Marcus
Bridgestone/Firestone	Nordstrom
Chico's	Office Depot
Claire's	Payless
Dillard's	Petrie's
Disney	PetSmart
Famous Footwear/ Naturalizer	Sears
The Gap	Target
JCPenney	Walgreens
Land's End	Wal-Mart

Working Part-Time

Working part-time or as a temporary employee is an excellent way of seeing if a particular company, or the retail industry generally, is for you. Because turnover is fairly high here, there are almost always openings. Getting a job is fairly easy. And there are openings in more areas than just cashiering or sales. During the busy seasons, retailers look for extra hands in stocking, driving, cleaning, assisting in visual merchandising, pricing, and tagging. If you have skills and experience, there

can also be temporary opportunities in management, information technology, public relations, accounting, marketing, and
advertising.

What Are the Advantages of Taking a Part-Time or Temporary Job?

- You get to see how a company really operates from the
  inside out without making a full-time commitment.
  You can also observe different departments within the
  company.
- You may be offered a permanent job.
- You get a chance to earn some extra cash and take
  advantage of the employee discount.
- You get the opportunity to update your skills in retail,
  which makes you more valuable in the marketplace.
- You get to meet new people and network. If there are no
  permanent positions available, but you do a great job
  and impress people, they may be able to help you find
  a full-time job at another company.

The disadvantages include:

- Temporary and part-time workers are the first to be let
  go in downturns.
- Temporaries and part timers have virtually no chances
  of advancement. The choice positions are generally
  offered to full-time employees first.

Getting
Hired

After an unpleasant experience in high school, Suzanne Meriden vowed she would never work retail again. She went on to college, where she studied international business and French. Meriden wasn't quite sure what she wanted to do with her life; she thought perhaps she would get a job that involved international travel or work at a company's corporate headquarters. She even considered becoming a teacher.

Then one day, a trashcan at her uncle's home changed her life. "I walked into my uncle's house, and he had the coolest trashcan I ever saw. I asked him where he got it, and he said, 'The Container Store in Costa Mesa.'" After a visit to that store, she became a customer.

Meriden graduated from college and took some time to ask herself what she really wanted. She began to research possibilities. "I read *Fortune* magazine in 2001 and noted that The Container Store was the number-one store to work for in America. But I never saw myself wearing an apron and talking to customers on the floor. I applied anyway, and I applied at other places as well. Then I had my first interview with a store manager, and I was amazed at how humble everyone was.

"One of the things he shared with me was that managers are expected to help clean the store bathrooms, and he asked me if this was something I could do. And I thought, yes, of course, because if I am going to ask someone to do something, I'd better be willing to do it myself. After several more interviews, I got an offer, but I still thought this would be a temporary job, maybe for a year."

Meriden's work experience was so positive that she completely changed her mind about retail. "In this age when technology is changing everything and moving you farther and farther away from people, retail gets you back with being in touch with people.

We are almost like therapists for our customers. We are helping them to organize their homes and if that brings happiness to them and allows them to spend more time with friends and family, that is great.

"I have always wanted to help people, and make my community a better place. And every time I put a smile on a customer's face, I feel that we've made the world a better place."

As a manager, Meriden says she works 48–49 hours per week, and that while every week is different, she spends at least 20 hours per week working on the floor with customers.

Meriden's job duties include hiring people to work in the store, and she discusses the skills she looks for in potential employees. "Many applicants come in and have great retail experience, but we just look at who you are. We want someone who can spend time with a happy customer, and with an unhappy customer as well. We don't want anyone to come in who wants to sell, but someone to help the customer solve a problem."

Meriden says that great listening skills are key. "We want someone to take the time to listen, and really hear what the problem is. We don't want to send you home with something you don't need. It's up to us to think outside the box and come up with a solution."

"You also need lots of energy to stand up all day. You are creating an air of excitement. You should come to work each day liking to come in and wanting to be with people and help people, because that's really what we do."

Meriden has the following advice for anyone considering a job in retail. "The *Fortune* 100 is a good starting guide. Take the time out and talk to current employees; look at the web site and ask questions. Ask yourself, 'Do I like the people here? Do I want to come in during the holidays? Am I going to be OK with being here the day after Christmas?' Follow your intuition. Does it feel right to you? Because it felt right for me to be here at The Container Store. I'm going to retire with this company."

■ ■ ■

So how do you go about finding the ideal place to work? This chapter talks about just that, as well as matching up your personal and professional goals. Once you've targeted potential employers, this chapter tells you how to create a winning resume.

Targeting Potential Employers

So how do you figure out where you want to work? One of the best ways to determine where you would be happy working is to ask friends and family who work in retail what they think about the companies they work for. Are they happy?

Why or why not? Would these same things make you happy, or unhappy?

You should also consider working for companies whose stores you enjoy frequenting. The most satisfied customers often make the best employees. If you are interested in getting a start in visual merchandising, find the store with the best visual displays, and apply.

This advice also works if you want a job at the headquarters of a retail company. If you enjoy the products the store carries, perhaps you'd enjoy being a part of the team at headquarters that makes your pleasurable store experience possible.

Another way to check companies out is by heading to the magazine rack in your local bookstore or library, or even to the internet. Each year, *Fortune* magazine publishes a list of the 100 best companies to work for. They arrive at this list by two means: their own evaluation of the policies and the culture of each company, and the opinions of the company's own employees. This list is a starting place for job seekers.

There are other groups that produce best companies to work for lists, using different criteria. *Working Mother* magazine creates an annual list of the top 100 places to work in which one of the criteria for inclusion is having a work environment that is friendly to working mothers. *Working Mother* cites companies that have come up with creative ways to encourage mothers to keep working, including allowing new mothers extended paid and unpaid leave or allowing employees to move to a part-time work schedule when family situations such as a new birth or caring for an elderly parent arise.

FORTUNE MAGAZINE'S 2007
10 BEST COMPANIES TO WORK FOR

1. Google
2. Genentech
3. Wegman's Food Market
4. Container Store
5. Whole Foods Market
6. Network Appliance
7. S. C. Johnson & Son
8. Boston Consulting Group
9. Methodist Hospital Systems
10. W. L. Gore & Associates

Source: *Fortune*, January 22, 2007.

It's important for you to decide what you want out of a job, and we'll talk about this again in Chapter 8. Just because a company's name appears on someone's list doesn't mean it's a good fit for *you*. Some of the companies that made *Fortune* magazine's "Best Companies to Work For" list have work environments featuring extremely long hours and high pressure. Obviously most of the employees are happy with this type of environment, or the company wouldn't have made the list. There are definitely people who thrive on pressure, and the rewards at these companies were significant. But if you are not one of those people, you are not going to be happy. So identify your wants and desires, and when doing your research, look for companies that are a match. Ask yourself which of the factors below are the most important to you:

- Having a job that allows me to have a life (work–life balance)
- Having a job where I can work hard and be rewarded for my efforts
- Making a difference
- Health-care benefits
- Child-care benefits
- Having a job that offers increased intellectual stimulation
- Having a job that offers interesting work
- Getting recognition
- Having power
- Working at a company where there isn't a lot of hierarchy
- Good pay
- A job where there are continuous opportunities for learning

Creating a Resume that Stands Out

Before we talk about what makes a great resume, let's talk about the purpose of a resume. The sole purpose of the resume is to get an interview. That's it. The resume is what prompts a potential employer to call you on the phone and schedule an interview. Then once you get your foot in the door, the resume may serve as the basis for discussion.

Length

One of the first questions many job-seekers ask is "How long should my resume be?" For most people, the resume should be a maximum of one to two pages. Remember that because the resume is accompanied by a cover letter, that adds an additional page of information for the potential employer to read. Most human resource professionals who are trying to make hiring decisions are extremely busy and do not want to read pages and pages of information about someone they don't even know. Human resource personnel estimate that they take, on average, *less than one minute* to review each resume that they receive. They simply don't have time to thoroughly examine everything. All the potential employer is trying to do in this preliminary phase is determine whether or not you are someone who should be invited for an interview.

Your Job Objective

The first step in creating a resume is creating your job objective. You need to be completely clear about the sort of job you want, and you should also have a clear understanding of the skills needed to do that job and which job experiences are relevant to it. Once you have determined your job objective, your entire resume will be built around that goal. If you are not completely certain about which job you want, narrow it down to two or three, and build one resume around each of those job objectives.

Experience

Let's say that you are graduating from college, and you want to apply for an executive training program for a retail company. Your eventual goal is to become a general manager. All during high school, you worked at your local ice cream shop. Should you include that experience? It depends. First of all, do you have other, more recent experience that is more closely related to your career goals? If so, list it first. That may take up all the available space. If there is still room, now should you include the ice cream job? Think about what skills you learned at that job that would be applicable in the job you want. Did you ever manage any shifts? Did you think up any ways to increase sales? Did you train new employees? All of these duties demonstrate skills that a store manager uses. So whatever you present on the resume, make it relevant to the job you are applying for.

Clarity

Another general rule for resumes is to be *clear* and *concise*. Again, you can talk up your experiences and skills in the interview, if that's what the employer wants to hear about. For now, make it short and sweet, and get the potential employer's attention. Use bullet points rather than long paragraphs. Highlight your strengths.

Use strong action verbs rather than verbs of being such as *was, were,* and *have been* in your resume. Strong action verbs include *created, presented, coordinated, accomplished, earned, facilitated, organized, managed, presented,* and *motivated.* Verbs of being don't create much excitement or get people's attention the way that verbs of action do.

White Space

When you are done with your resume, make sure there is white space on the page. White space is the open area of the paper, the portion of the page that is not covered in words. If the words of your resume are completely crowding the page and there isn't much white space, it is less appealing for the human resource employee to read. Resumes with white space spread meaningfully around the page invite readers into the text.

Here's a trick that graphic designers often use: print off a draft copy of your resume and look at the resume upside down, without actually reading the words. This will give you a fresh look at the document, and perhaps a better idea of how someone else will see it. Is the format pleasing to the eye? Does it look crowded, or is there a good use of white space? Also, don't use any font smaller than 10 point, or any unusual, difficult-to-read fonts.

Highlight Accomplishments

Use numbers and concrete examples to highlight your accomplishments. For example, "Worked hard and beat expected sales quota regularly" sounds OK, but "Doubled sales quota for four consecutive quarters" sounds much more impressive.

Addresses

Nowadays people include their e-mail addresses as well as their physical address on their resumes, and you should, too. Just make sure that if your current e-mail address is not particularly professional sounding, you create a new one.

Proofread—and Proofread Again

Finally, whatever you do, proofread your resume before sending it out. Recruiters who see resumes that are sloppy or contain grammatical or spelling errors will assume that because the candidate didn't care enough to submit a decent resume, he or she probably will not care about the quality of his or her work either. There's no excuse for not submitting a perfect resume because it's something over which the candidate has complete control. Read your resume and cover letter out loud; professional proofreaders often read documents out loud to catch errors. *Do not* under any circumstances depend on your word processor to catch mistakes. Word processing programs are notorious for occasionally making incorrect corrections. Also, if you type "there" when you meant "their," your word processor will not catch this, or similar, mistakes. Have a friend with outstanding written communication skills proof your work as well.

Getting
Ahead

PROFILE
Allison Trembly
Whole Foods Market
Lakewood, Colorado

Sometimes your dream job is right in front of you, in your very own company, just waiting for you to claim it. Allison Trembly is a store marketing director for Whole Foods Market in Lakewood, Colorado, who did just that, working her way up from cashier to a top position in the company.

"I've always worked retail. When I was a Girl Scout, I did the cookie sales. Then when I was in high school, I worked in malls, at

JCPenney and Montgomery Ward. I worked to get money for shoes, or whatever I needed. Then I worked at IHOP for a year as a line cook. I realized that I couldn't keep on, because I wanted to start making real money so I could own a car and a house, get married, and have kids, but I couldn't do that on the money I was making.

"So I went to college. I wanted to be a teacher. When I got out, I worked for one year and found it was not for me. I moved on to Goodwill Industries, where I did community relations work. I liked educating people. I met some people at that job, and one asked me to come and do this same sort of work for the mayor's office in Austin, Texas. I loved it, but I got homesick for Colorado. I decided to go back and go to graduate school. One of my clients at the time was Whole Foods Market, and a representative offered me a job at the Denver location as a cashier while I went to school."

Trembly accepted the position, moved back to the Denver area, and started graduate school. She was working at Whole Foods and going to graduate school full time, working towards a master's degree in communication management. "I planned to work at an advertising agency when I was done. All of my peers in graduate school were already working at great jobs and making tons of money while they went to school part time. I felt a little funny because I was just a cashier, but on the other hand, my classmates were a bit jealous about how much fun I was having at work."

Trembly worked hard, and her efforts were noticed and rewarded. "I went from being a cashier and bagger to being the supervisor of the front end." A front-end supervisor is responsible for all the cashiers and baggers for an entire shift. "On top of that, I volunteered, and planned store parties, etc. Eventually I became the body care buyer. This person takes care of buying anything to do with body care, such as shampoo, conditioner, lotions, nutrition, toothpaste, and even incense and candles."

Trembly's plans of working for an advertising agency were changed abruptly by a change in her outlook. "I was working the Blues Festival in Telluride for Whole Foods. While there I heard that the Boulder store, which at the time was the number-one store in the company, had an opening for a store marketing director. At that point, my outlook towards Whole Foods changed from 'this is a job' to 'this is a career.'"

Going back to Boulder was a natural for Trembly, who grew up in the area. "I was at the Boulder store for two years. As store marketing director, I was able to help out the nonprofits who helped me out as a kid, and even my high school. During this time I did other exciting things as well, such as opening stores in Colorado Springs and Ft. Collins. Every time I asked Whole Foods to let me do something a little bit different, they always said yes. It was like I was writing my own job description."

The position of store marketing director varies from store to store at Whole Foods, and the job is built into each store. The store marketing director is responsible for promoting the store presence in local community events, as well as promoting merchandise within the stores. For example, the store may have a booth set up at a local festival. Trembly explains, "We like to be grass roots and work in our community. Within the store, the store marketing director may motivate teams to do tastings and other events, and to get engaged with the customers."

Trembly believes that it is important to move around to prevent becoming stagnant. So when the Belmar store in Lakewood, Colorado, was in the building phase, she took a look inside what was then an enormous, 65,000-square-foot shell. "I knew this would be an amazing store, and it was only seven miles from my house. I applied for the store marketing director position along with 82 others, and was thrilled when I got the job. We opened the store in December.

"When I started at Whole Foods, there were only two locations in Colorado, and now there are seven. We are now big enough to be our own region. I had no idea when I was a cashier in graduate school that this would be my career."

"Gratification comes from giving back to the community. Whole Foods is my family. We have store parties, golf tournaments, even a softball team." When Trembly's real family saw how happy she was, they were inspired to become a part of the Whole Foods experience. "My younger brother went to work in the meat department in the Boulder store when he got out of the army. Now he is the assistant manager. And my little sister works at Whole Foods when she is on break from college. My dad even bought stock in the company. This is not just a job, but a lifestyle.

"Sometimes you have to sit still, see if what you are doing feels right, and if it does, go with it. I see so many young people who want to be president right now, but you have to start on the front line, cashiering, bagging, etc. And even when you do move up, you still need to work the front lines now and then to stay in touch with your audience."

■ ■ ■

Not very many people would consider taking a vacation and not having any sort of a plan for where they were going, where they were going to stay when they arrived, or what they were going to do. Having no plan at all could mean pulling up to a hotel with no vacancies or rates that are so high as to be unaffordable.

The same logic about needing a plan can be applied to just about any venture in life, but it's especially important when it comes to your career. You don't want to find yourself

working in one position for some time, only to find yourself getting passed over for promotion time and time again
because you are not qualified for a position with more responsibility. It could be that in order to get a promotion, you need
to further your education or enhance your skill set. A plan
helps you see what work you need to do. You've got to have
a plan, or else you might just find yourself nowhere.

So just how do you come up with a career path? If you are
still in college or just getting out, you might think you don't
have enough experience to make an intelligent decision about
what you want to do with your life. And that's OK. Good,
solid plans can be tweaked along the way as you find out
more about yourself.

Self-Assessment

The first step in creating a career plan is to do a thorough self-
assessment. It is important to be totally honest with yourself.
Who are you and what are you looking for in life? First, think
about all the times you have experienced happiness. What are
the things you enjoy doing? Do you enjoy spending time with
other people? Do you like doing things by yourself? Or, do you
like a combination of both? Also ask yourself about money.
Would you be happy working in a job you truly enjoyed but
didn't pay much money?

Then think about the times in your life when you have
been successful, and try to figure out what skills you brought
to the situation. Are you good at giving presentations? Are

you a whiz at solving puzzles? Do your friends always come to you for advice in how to handle their relationships with peers or co-workers? Were you able to manage a difficult person at work or school? Assess your communication skills, your analytical abilities, your people skills, and your creativity. What skills do you need to improve?

Finally, assess your values. This is probably the most critical self-assessment question. If you are working with people who do not share your values, you may wind up miserable. Valerie C. works in the headquarters of a company as a designer. She has held this position for a number of years, and though she doesn't make a huge salary, she is proud of her work and dedicated to constantly improving her craft. Some of the recently hired designers do not share her values and feel that it is perfectly acceptable to take drawings they find on the internet and pass them off as their own to upper management. Being associated with a group of people who do not share Valerie's values and integrity has made Valerie unhappier than anything she has ever encountered in her entire career.

Explore Career Possibilities

After you have completed your self-assessment, explore different careers. Reading this book is a great start. You should also ask friends and family if they are happy with their jobs and what they like or dislike about their work. If you are still in school, talk with faculty members and your guidance department. They may be able to recommend a path you had not considered before. And sometimes it helps to talk to total strangers. If you are considering a career in retail, the next time you go shopping and notice an employee who is doing a great job, ask that employee if he or she enjoys the job and why. Happy people love talking about their work. The goal in this part of the exercise is to find a good career fit for someone with your skill set and values.

Choosing a Path

Once you decide on a certain career, creating a path for advancement is the easy part. Let's say you decide you've assessed your skills and values, done your research, and feel that being a buyer would be a good fit for you. Most large companies have career paths for each area within the company. Figure 8.1 gives a typical career path for a buyer in a large retail company.

Strategy of Alternating

The career path chart in Figure 8.1 demonstrates another means of getting ahead—the strategy of alternating. Once you get into a retail operation that is bigger than a few stores, you will have the store environment and the headquarters environment. If you want to reach the upper levels of the company, you should know what working in the store is all about, and if you are going to be in store management, you should understand how things work at headquarters so you can get what you need to run your store.

FIGURE **8.1: BUYER CAREER PATH**

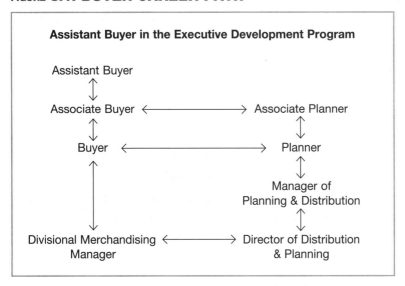

Assistant Buyer in the Executive Development Program

Store managers, divisional managers, vice presidents, and other high-ranking executives often have diversified experience, gaining experience in different departments of the store and home office, which makes terrific sense on a practical level. Perhaps the store manager has put in some time in the home office, starting out as an assistant buyer and then working in many different departments in the store. This gives the store manager an idea of what's important to those in corporate as well as a greater understanding of how each of the parts of the organization functions. The store manager can run the entire store more effectively and efficiently with this knowledge.

Staying Away from Crabs

George Colombo is president and founder of George Colombo International, a sought-after speaker, consultant, and author, and an expert in the customer relationship management industry. Colombo advises retail employees to stay away from crabs. "There's a great story about retail. If you have a big pail of crabs and one crab tries to escape, the other crabs will pull him back. If you are working retail, there's a better than average chance you are going to meet some people with bad attitudes. It's hard sometimes to not be surrounded by people with bad attitudes. But if you are serious about building a career in retail, you must be vigilant about not getting caught up in this stuff. This is your career, and you have to transcend the negativity."

Start-Ups and Turnarounds

There are certain individuals who specialize in start-ups and turnarounds, and for those who are successful at this specialty, their value as employees skyrockets. If you can ramp up a new store and move it into the profitable segment quickly, your career will progress quickly. Likewise, if you can turn around a store that is marginal or in danger of being shut down, you will be a tremendous asset to any organization.

TEN TIPS TO SUCCESS
IN THE RETAIL INDUSTRY

Congratulations! You've landed a job with a great
company. Now what are you going to do? Make
plans for your future, of course. Where do you want to be next year?
How about in five years? Start planning your future now, with the
following ten tips on succeeding in the retail industry:

1. *Be a team player.* No one enjoys working with a back stabber,
   or someone who is jealous when others get ahead, or worst of
   all, a whiner. If you find yourself complaining constantly about
   the company where you work, do yourself and everyone around
   you a favor and move on. Also, treat everyone with respect. The
   person you just snubbed in the elevator may turn out to be the
   CEO's secretary, or maybe even your next boss.

2. *Be a friend.* Network within your company and within your
   industry. Meet as many people as you can and consider working
   with others on projects.

3. *Be a student.* If you want to move up, start learning the duties
   of the position you desire. For example, watch how your boss
   handles difficult customers. Or ask your boss if you can learn
   how to budget, how to create schedules, etc. Remember to
   dress the part as well.

4. *Be a teacher.* Groom those who work for you to take your job. It's good for you, and good for the company. One of the marks of a great manager is that when she or he is out of the store or office, things run smoothly because that manager has trained the staff so effectively. Some supervisors horde important information or do not train their staffs, thinking that the company will find them indispensable. This strategy is not only selfish, but can backfire as well. Sometimes these managers are actually held back from promotion because there is no one qualified to take his or her place.

5. *Be flexible.* If the company asks you to move to another store or city, give it careful consideration. If the company asks you to take a lateral move that will give you experience in another department, jump on it. The more versatile your skill set, the more marketable you become.

6. *Be strategic.* Just as companies have the one-year and five-year plans, so should you. Create a yearly plan complete with career objectives and how you are going to achieve them. Do you need to further your education or attend special training? Identify these needs and create a plan to advance your skills. Share this with your boss, and get his or her opinion on your plan.

7. *Be a good listener.* If you hear that someone is leaving or a new position is being created, get on it before someone else does.

8. *Be a good observer.* Look around your company and see what's working and what isn't. If you work in a store, make it a point to visit departments other than your own and see what you can learn. Visit your competition—what's working for them? What isn't? Read financial publications and trade publications to get a jump on the latest trends.

9. *Be proactive.* Don't wait for the higher-ups to point out problems to you and ask you to fix them. If you see something in the store or in your office that can be improved upon, by all means take the initiative and see what you can do to fix that problem. Show that you are paying attention to what's going on around you and that you care about your company, your peers, and your customers. It may not be your job to pick up a piece of litter in the aisle, but do it anyway before someone slips on it and gets hurt.

10. *Be ambitious.* It's good for you and good for your company for you to want to get ahead. Set reasonable goals, and discuss them with your boss. Perhaps she or he can offer suggestions on how to achieve these goals.

Doing It
on Your Own

Wells opened the HoundsTooth Bakery nearly two years ago, prompted to do so by a family event. "A few years ago I went to my sister's 50th birthday celebration, and it dawned on me then that there had to be more to it than going to work for a paycheck. I had worked in corporate life for 17 years, and during the last few years I had shopped at a boutique for my own pets.

"So I combined my knowledge of accounting, retail, and my love of animals, and started developing the idea of opening my own pet bakery. I was fortunate that the woman whose store I had been shopping in had a training program and that she sold me her recipes. I went to many other stores and tasted all their products.

"The hardest thing to overcome was finding a retail space. The area of town where I wanted to locate was a place that didn't have a lot of retail space. It was by my house, but there was nothing within about ten miles.

"So I spent seven months every weekend and many evenings driving around looking for a retail spot. I started expanding the search area, and I found an older location, so the rent was less expensive and it was located next to a doggie day care and boarding business. The bonus was that it was located right on one of the busiest roads in Winter Park, with lots of drive-by business. Visibility and word-of-mouth are key to a small retail business."

Wells stresses that owning your own business is hard work. "I'm almost always here an hour before opening, and I seldom leave before closing time. The first year I worked a lot of Sundays, even though we were closed. Being closed allows you to get a lot of work done that you cannot do while customers are in the store, like mopping up. It's a huge commitment, and for your family as well. There are long days, and you never sit down. I work probably 65–70 hours a week, depending on what's going on."

Another consideration in opening your own business is that you may have to forego a paycheck during the start-up period. Wells explains, "I haven't had a paycheck since I left my other job because I roll any extra money back into the business. I should be able to start taking home a paycheck at the two-year mark. People think you open a store and sell stuff and the money goes into your pocket. That's not what happens. You have to find another means of income until the store starts making money. We are able to do that because we had savings and investments.

"My original investment was $110,000. I used $64,000 to cover the opening for things like paint, flooring, merchandise, display equipment, a cash register, cooking equipment, permitting, and everything you need to open the door. I also got a $50,000 SBA [Small Business Administration] loan for operating cash. The biggest reason that small businesses fail is not from a lack of business, but from a lack of capital. The first money that you take in has to purchase new merchandise to sell and cover operating expenses."

Wells figured out the most effective means of advertising for her particular business through trial and error. "Advertising was incredibly more expensive than I expected, and phenomenally less effective that I had hoped for. The majority of our success is through word-of-mouth and putting samples at vet's offices. I bake a treat, heat seal it along with a business card, and that works wonderfully. Networking through similar businesses such as groomers, pet-sitters, and trainers is great—you send them business, and they send you business."

So is all the hard work worth it to Wells? "Oh gosh yeah," she responds enthusiastically. Wells says that the best part of the owning your own business is clearly the customers. "When the customers come in, they are shopping for someone they love unconditionally. You never get a customer in a bad mood, because they are buying something they want to buy. You also have the pleasure of being able to make decisions without all the corporate red tape.

"The best advice I can give you about opening your own business is that if you think about it too much, you'll never do it. That's not to say you shouldn't think about it—it's a matter of do you have the guts to do it?"

■ ■ ■

Many people dream about starting their own business and becoming their own boss. Running your own business can be the most rewarding thing you ever do in your professional life, but it can also mean losing your life's savings if you don't know what you're in for. How can you tell if becoming a business owner is right for you? Take the following quiz to see if opening your own business is really a good fit for you and your lifestyle.

FIGURE 9.1: **QUIZ: DO YOU HAVE WHAT IT TAKES TO RUN YOUR OWN BUSINESS?**

Instructions: Read each question, and check the answer that best describes your feelings. Most importantly, be honest.

1. Do you usually take the initiative in situations?
   a. I always seem to figure out what to do. No one has to tell me.
   b. Sometimes other people need to tell me what to do, and sometimes I figure it out myself.
   c. I have a hard time figuring out what I should do next.

2. Do you like being with other people?
   a. I like meeting new people and can relate to most everyone, even people who are very different from me.
   b. I already have enough friends.
   c. Stupid people really annoy me.

FIGURE 9.1: QUIZ: DO YOU HAVE WHAT IT TAKES TO RUN YOUR OWN BUSINESS? CONT.

3. Are you a take-charge person?

   a. I am perfectly comfortable telling people what needs to be done, and people never seem to mind it when I do.

   b. I can give the orders if someone else lets me know what needs to be done.

   c. I don't like being a bossy person.

4. How do you feel about making decisions?

   a. I am very good at making decisions, and the results are almost always good.

   b. I like to have input from others and plenty of time to make decisions.

   c. I am not comfortable making decisions.

5. Are you financially able to go without a paycheck for up to two years?

   a. I have saved enough money to go without a paycheck for two years.

   b. I have a little in savings, but not enough for two years.

   c. I am the wage earner in my family, so I'll need a paycheck each month.

6. Do you have expertise in the type of business you wish to open?

   a. Yes, I have worked in this field for several years in different positions, so I really know how to run this type of business.

   b. I have worked in business for several years, but not in the type of store I would like to open.

   c. No, I don't have any experience working in the type of store I am planning on opening.

7. **Are you comfortable taking responsibility?**

    a. I like being in charge and others are comfortable with me as the leader.

    b. I can be in charge if necessary, but I like for someone else to be in charge sometimes.

    c. I don't like being responsible because that means you get blamed when things go wrong.

8. **Are you a hard worker?**

    a. I am willing to work hard to make my dream come true.

    b. I don't mind working hard for a bit, but when I get tired, I like to stop.

    c. I do not want to work more than 40 hours per week.

9. **Are you well organized?**

    a. I think it's imperative to have a very detailed business plan. That way we are all on the same page, and everyone understands where we are going.

    b. I'll stay on the plan unless things get too confused.

    c. Plans are boring. I'm more of a free spirit and prefer to go with the flow.

10. **How good is your health?**

    a. I'm in top shape, exercise regularly, and take good care of myself. That's probably why I have so much energy.

    b. My health is about average.

    c. I get tired pretty easily and seem to need a nap every so often.

FIGURE 9.1: QUIZ: DO YOU HAVE WHAT IT TAKES TO RUN YOUR OWN BUSINESS? CONT.

11. Do people usually trust you?

    a. My word is my bond. I don't make promises I cannot keep.

    b. I try to be honest as much as possible, but sometimes it's hard keeping your word because the situation changes.

    c. I think it's important to do or say whatever you need to in order to make a go of your business. Besides, all those big shots on Wall Street lie all the time and look how rich they are.

12. Are you able to stick with your goals?

    a. Once I make a commitment, I'll do everything within my power to achieve that goal.

    b. I almost always finish what I start out to do if everything goes well.

    c. I think it's important to bail when you see things are not going to work out.

13. Is your family supportive of you opening your own business?

    a. My husband is completely supportive and understands that I will not be bringing in any income at first, and that I will be working evenings, Sundays, and even some holidays.

    b. My husband says it's OK with him.

    c. My wife says I should do whatever I want, as long as the money keeps coming in and our lifestyle doesn't change.

14. Why do you want to go into business for yourself?

    a. I've always dreamed of opening this sort of business, and through research I've determined there is a real need for it in my area.

FIGURE 9.1: QUIZ: DO YOU HAVE WHAT IT TAKES TO RUN YOUR OWN BUSINESS? CONT.

b. I think it would be fun to not have a boss.

c. I'm sick and tired of working 9 to 5, my boss is a monster, and on top of everything, my job is a bore. It would be great to do what I want to do for a change.

15. Do you realize that you could lose your life's savings?

a. Yes, I've thought about it and discussed it with my family. It's a risk we are willing to take.

b. Yes, I've thought about it. My husband would not be happy if he knew how much is at stake.

c. What? Everything? You've got to be kidding! Maybe I'd better think this over.

Now add up all the times you checked "a" as your answer, "b" as your answer, and "c" as your answer. If most of your answers are "a," then you have probably given careful consideration to the risks involved in opening your own business and are better prepared than most. If many of your answers are "b," then consider going into business with a partner who can help you with business expertise and decision making, or consider buying a franchise. Look for a partner whose skill set complements your own. If most of your answers were "c," you should rethink going into business for yourself, because more than likely not even a partner would be able to save you.

A CLOTHING BOUTIQUE

Shelley Petrilli owns a women's clothing boutique in a small town in Colorado. She talks about how she selected the location for her business. "It wasn't my number-one choice, but it boiled down to finances. I was able to afford it and avoid astronomical rent when I was first starting out. This is a small town, and it's hard to find a good location."

Although the downtown area is the heart of the town and a great haven for tourists, the shops are quite small and Petrilli wanted a bit more space, so she located her business elsewhere. Her choice in location also influenced her choices in pricing. "My goal was to make people feel like they could afford to come in, and come in more frequently."

Picking a Niche

Niche marketing refers to serving a specialized yet profitable corner of the market. It is impossible to be all things to all people, and it doesn't make good business sense to try. Your greatest chance of succeeding in opening a business is to offer a product or service that is unique in a market that needs what you are selling.

The potential business owner must identify his or her ideal customer. Once the entrepreneur figures out who this customer is, then he or she can make the right product, sales, and marketing decisions. Look around you. What do you as a consumer, as a family member, or as a hobbyist notice is lacking in your current marketplace?

The best businesses come from someone's passions. Opening a business is extremely hard work, and you need to believe in the worthiness of your endeavor with all your heart in order to sustain you in difficult times. Think about your skills, interests, and background, what product you could be excited about providing, and what market you would be enthusiastic serving. When you find the ideal niche, it gives you an overwhelming advantage over your competition and your fledgling business a better chance at succeeding.

Location, Location, Location

The location you select for your new enterprise is so important that it can be the determining factor in whether your business succeeds or fails. Again, you need to know the profile of your potential customers, and plop your business right down in front of them, in the paths they travel each day.

Once you determine ideal locations, cost must be factored in. The mall may be ideal, but fledgling businesses rarely can afford the rent. Also, if you plan on hiring employees, is your potential location one that would attract and keep good employees? Is there adequate parking available for your customers? Is safety an issue? Is the location you are considering zoned for the business you'd like to open?

Getting Financing

The first step in starting your own business is to create a detailed business plan. The business plan will be reviewed by investors or banks to determine if your idea for a business is worth funding. Potential funders want to see the financial projections you create. At what point will the business begin to turn a profit? How much are you investing? Will you be able to live without a paycheck until the business is profitable? Investors also evaluate your marketing strategies, which include your plans for advertising and promoting the new business.

Where can you go for financing? You have three realistic options:

1. Borrow the money from friends or family
2. Apply for a loan from a bank
3. Apply for a loan from the U.S. Small Business Administration

Let's talk about asking friends and/or family for a loan. Should you pursue this route, make certain you and your friends or family have a written agreement regarding the loan. Thoroughly review your business plan with them. Will they have ownership in your new business in return for the loan? Will they have any say in how the business is run? And when can they expect the loan to be repaid? A written agreement will spell out what's expected on both sides and hopefully prevent misunderstandings.

You can always apply for a loan from a bank. The bank's main concern is whether or not the business has the potential to repay the loan, along with the interest. You need to have collateral to cover the loan, and oftentimes the lending institution will expect you to keep your business accounts with them. Finally, you can consult with your local Small Business Administration (SBA). The SBA is a government agency whose mission is to promote and aid small businesses. One of their mission statements reads: "We empower the spirit of entrepreneurship within every community to promote and realize the American dream." The SBA has three different loan programs. Again, be prepared to discuss your business plan in detail with your local agency. The SBA wants you to have available your personal financial statements, collateral available to secure the loan, the management resumes of all involved in operating the business, assumptions used in your projected earnings statements, and the pro-forma balance sheets showing what the business would look like if the loan were granted.

Floor Planning

You also need to determine the floor plan for the store. Before you start to determine the particulars, what is your vision for your store? Do you have an idea of how you want to the store to look? Who are your competitors and how will your store be different? Will your merchandise require special fixtures or display cases? Do you need any special permits if you are going to modify the structure? Don't forget to think about paint, flooring, special equipment, cash registers, the ceiling, and finally, the all-important lighting.

Manufacturers

How fast does the merchandise arrive? How and when do you reorder? When do you start realizing quantity discounts? You'll need to have a full understanding of the financial and delivery arrangements with all of the suppliers of your merchandise, or you'll have nothing to sell.

PROFILE

Lyle Davis, Specialty Retailer
Pastures of Plenty
Longmont, Colorado

Operating a kiosk in several farmer's markets where he sells stunningly beautiful organic flowers and produce is just one of Lyle Davis' businesses. He also operates a small family farm where he grows all that he sells, in addition to running a thriving catering business. He talks about how he came to develop the expertise necessary to run his own business as well as what's different about kiosk marketing.

"When I was in my late 20s, and having no previous business experience, I went into business with a couple of friends; one of them did have retail experience. And I had come from a family in New York with a gourmet food background, a family that really took great joy in gathering. My role was the 'foodie,' and I developed all the

---

produce and food service lines. I was not so much the money guy, or the financier. Way before Wild Oats, we were one of the original natural supermarkets, bridging with organic.

"That business, Alfalfa's Markets, grew into a 13-store chain grossing about $100 million per year. We carried things like smoked fish, the same sort of merchandise you would find at Balducci's in New York."

But things changed dramatically for Davis in 1996. "Alfalfa's was 70 percent venture capitalized, and the investors decided they wanted to sell. It forced a bidding war for the company between Wild Oats and Whole Foods, with Wild Oats eventually winning."

Davis did not regret the change. "After 18 years of retail, I felt that it was time for me to make a change. I was never much of a corporate guy anyway. I was ready to go, so the timing was good. I had started my farm, Pastures of Plenty, in 1993, and in 1996 I took the farm to a different level.

"We offer a field-to-table experience. My wife and I celebrate it all. When I was in the process of stepping up the farm, someone I knew requested that I do the food for a large party. Turned out to be for Ferrari International, and we were to prepare lunch for three days and serve 300–400 people each day. My partner and I were successful, and we made great money. I created the field-to-table experience that had been my dream."

So what made Davis consider going into kiosk marketing? "The farm takes up most of my time. Because I had extensive produce experience, it was quickly apparent to me that if you were going to have a small, boutique type of farm I would need to get retail prices for my goods. I thought about a roadside stand near the farm, but my farm is not located where a roadside stand would work.

"So I thought about a niche. I chose flowers because not as many people are selling them. Plus, there's the 'bend-over' factor to consider. With most vegetables, you've got to bend over, pick the vegetable,and clean it up in order to get it to market. And we do a whole line of specialty vegetables, niche items. But with flowers, all you have to do is cut them, and they are ready to go.

"There are all different types of farmer's markets. There's the flea-market type where farmers are in selling with other sorts of businesses, like people who make jewelry. If you are willing to pay the dues and the managers let you in, you are set. In some of the other markets you basically have to grow all your own stuff, and it's free to participate.

"Farmer's markets are very much about developing personal relationships. People love the idea of buying from the owner, from the producer of the product. You've got to have the willingness to be the spokesperson and to meet your customer.

"Location can be a trial-and-error sort of thing, or it can be instinct. I am selling flowers, so I obviously do better in the farmer's markets where the people have higher incomes, because you have to have disposable income to buy flowers. There is a certain obviousness to where you sell.

"My customer is predominately female. You have to have a sense of the profile of your customer as well.

"I am always looking at fine-tuning. After this year, I'm looking at the mountain markets, but that means I need a new truck. The farmer's market kiosk is always changing. It is much different from ten years ago. The economy was such that people were spending more. Also, a lot of people have tried to open their own farmer's markets, and that tends to erode the real farmer's markets.

"In order to succeed, you have to have that personality, flexibility, and the backbone to deal with the ebbs and flows.

"Small family farms tend to make very little money. With most of them, one of the spouses is probably working to bring in a steadier income. But you get a beautiful place to live, and a great place to raise a family."

Kiosk Retailing

Kiosk retailing usually refers to the open carts found in malls, airports, theme parks, or other high-traffic areas where people sell merchandise. Vendors may also sell newspapers, coffee or other refreshments, or even tickets from kiosks. Kiosks may also be self-service, such as photo kiosks, but this discussion is limited to the open carts.

In the retail industry, selling from kiosks is referred to as *specialty retailing*.

With kiosk marketing, the good news is that your risk isn't as high as it is if you had started a full-sized store, because it doesn't cost as much to enter the marketplace. The rent is lower, you don't need as much inventory, and fixtures are not required. Of course you can still lose your entire investment, but because it doesn't cost as much to start up in the first place, you obviously would not lose as much money. Options in kiosk marketing can include deciding everything yourself—what to carry and how much to charge—to turnkey operations where you pay extra for the entire operation to be set up for you, almost like a franchise.

While the physical structure of the kiosk is small, you still need to do your homework before opening the business—figuring out if you are going into business for the right reasons and determining if you have the proper support system and the financial resources to sustain you while you are starting out. You need to come up with a business plan, which details your plan for the business. More than likely the leasing manager at the mall or airport where you wish to do business will want to review your plan before he or she allows you to rent a cart or a kiosk. The leasing manager must be convinced that there is a real demand for the product or products you wish to sell from your kiosk.

Location, as we talked about before, is absolutely critical. Specialty retailing on carts and kiosks is all about impulse buying, much more so than buying in most stores. Many impulses begin with *seeing*, and obviously carts and kiosks are easily seen because they are located directly in the flow of traffic. Kiosks have an advantage over stores in this area because they have incredible visibility. So clearly you need to know the profile of the person who is likely to buy your product and where that person is likely to shop. You must match the market with the product in order to succeed.

Impulse buying requires disposable income, so if your product costs $50 and the people in your market cannot afford that, then you need to think about locating in another area. Likewise, you should be concerned about *where* in the mall you locate your cart or kiosk. If you sell products that appeal to teens, you'd be better off in front of the video game store than near a department store.

What Products Should I Sell at My Kiosk?

People generally sell items at carts and kiosks that have tremendous visual appeal. The product, like the cart itself, should capture the customer's attention immediately. Experts in shopping behavior have determined that people purchase items either to solve a problem or for pleasure. Think of marketing your product to do one or the other. The most popular specialty retail products fall into the following categories:

- *Impulse items.* Generally inexpensive, this category includes so many products that it is impossible to list them all. An abbreviated list is cosmetics, bath and body products, inexpensive jewelry such as charms, candles, flowers, incense, candy, foods, hats, calendars, ties, mugs, key chains, accessories, aromatherapy products, and photo frames.

- *The new hot item.* Are you good at predicting what the latest trend is going to be? If so, this may be your chance to cash in. Remember the wildly popular Beanie Babies by Ty? Trends can either be short term or long.

- *Personalized items.* Personalized items appeal to almost everyone, because they are difficult to come by. A favorite item for personalization is Christmas ornaments. Items for babies are especially popular, and include personalized photo frames, bibs, hats, sweaters, and even wooden block letters spelling out the child's name.

- *Collectibles.* This category includes action figures, diecast models, trading cards, plush toys, and such. In order to be successful with these items, the retailer must have in-depth product knowledge.

- *Licensed merchandise.* Selling licensed merchandise requires having an agreement with a company (the licensor) granting permission to sell the product. The Disney Company is a prime example of a company involved in licensed merchandise.

- *Seasonal or holiday.* Many kiosk product lines revolve around Christmas, but other holidays are popular as well. Some kiosks sell masks for Halloween, candy or flowers for Valentine's Day, and so on.
- *Demonstration products.* These goods require salespeople to have complete knowledge of the product and be able to demonstrate all of the features effectively. Demonstrating a product is one of the most effective means of selling. Examples include wind-up toys, remote control cars, and a massager.
- *Handcrafted items.* The best thing about handcrafted merchandise is that it is unique. Some people spend most of the year crafting merchandise that will be sold over the course of a couple of months at a holiday kiosk.
- *Themed merchandise.* If you think long and hard, you can come up with a theme for your kiosk. For example, there have been successful businesses built around a science fiction theme, a comic book theme, or an international theme, such as merchandise from Ireland.

Other Kiosk Considerations

Specialty retailers are especially vulnerable to theft because it is impossible to keep an eye on all four sides of the cart and oftentimes there is only one salesperson working a shift. The vast majority of these retailers reportedly do not have insurance covering theft. Employee theft and after-hours theft are also huge problems.

Be aware that most malls require businesses to purchase liability and property damage insurance.

PROFILE

Rene MacLeod, Franchise Owner
Barnie's, Winter Springs, Florida

It's been just over two years since two couples got together and decided to go into business for themselves. Rather than go totally on their own, they opted to go through a well-known franchise and opened a Barnie's Coffee and Tea store. Rene MacLeod, one of the owners, serves as the general manager of the store. She explains the group's reasoning. "We wanted to try something independently, and all four of us were interested in opening a business. We felt that a coffee shop would be perfect, so we began looking at different opportunities.

"We went with a franchise, which basically means you are using the company's brands, their names, and their products. While you are giving up some control, you are also making it easier on yourself because you have a built-in clientele. So a lot of our market-

---

ing centers around letting people know you are there, and not so much around the product, because so many people already know the product."

Barnie's is an Orlando-based company, and before MacLeod's group made their decision, they did quite a bit of research. "We all live here in Winter Springs, just five minutes away from the store. This area clearly needed this type of business, and there are not that many coffee franchises available. So we visited just about all the Barnie's stores in the area and looked at the way they were set up and run. They had a good customer base, the stores seemed always busy with a good following, and their customers seemed happy.

"The other thing that impressed us at the time was that Barnie's seemed pretty flexible. They were willing to make some concessions. For example, we wanted to have a bit of a different look, which they allowed. They wanted us to use their logo, cafe scene and sign, but they did let us have some individuality. Not everything has to be the same."

MacLeod and her partners came up with an arrangement that would further lessen the risk inherent in opening your own business. "While all four of us work in the store, our arrangement was that everyone kept his or her day job except for me, and I agreed to manage the store on a daily basis. This means I am pretty much in charge of the staff, hiring, inventory, and everything that has to do with the daily operation of a store.

"None of us had retail experience, although we had managerial experience in other fields. One of us is an engineer, another a Realtor, another has a business degree, and I was in nursing management. This was another reason we went with a franchise experience, because they provided training, and they were there for support after we opened. They gave us product training, so we are all well versed in that. Barnie's sent us to train with their managers, and I learned from them how to inventory, and all about staffing and customer service."

The group also had a specific location in mind for their new venture, the Winter Springs Town Center, which is a new community of shops, restaurants, and offices. "The location fit with what we wanted to do with our shop, a lifestyle center, a hometown kind of coffee shop that is going to be the heart of Winter Springs. We felt this had the most potential for the shop to do well."

MacLeod has great advice for those considering opening their own franchises. "If you are looking at a franchise, look at their training program and how good it is based on your experience. While my group certainly had plenty of business experience, we were not experienced in retail. Most franchises do have training programs, and they vary in length.

"Definitely look into the corporate structure, how the company is run, what their ideas are about the future, and their philosophy, and compare it all with yours. If you are going in a different direction, you may not want to go with that company."

MacLeod also discussed what it's like to run your own business. "I think it's important to have a lot of life experience before opening your own business to make certain it's the step you want to take. You put in a lot of hours, sweat, and tears. I started out working 70–80 hours when we first opened, and now I am down to about 50–55, and that includes my nonscheduled time. You are pretty much on call 24 hours per day. If something breaks, you are the one who has to fix it.

"Small business usually take two to three years before they start making a profit, so you need to have two to three years of working capital to cover that period."

Even though it's been difficult, MacLeod relishes her experience. "This has been fun and allowed me to be creative with gift baskets and catering. Even though it's a challenge, it's something new, and we've met some great people."

To Franchise or Not to Franchise

Let's start off by discussing what is meant by the term *franchise*. Franchise can be thought of as a business relationship between a company that wishes to distribute its services or products and a person who wishes to run his or her own business. The company that sells the rights to offer its products or services is known as the *franchisor*, while the person buying these rights is called the *franchisee*.

In 2003, the International Franchise Association participated in a study designed to determine the importance of franchises in the American economy. The study found that franchising generates jobs for more than 18 million Americans, and accounts for 10 percent of the private sector economy. The study also revealed that more industries are choosing franchising as a means of expanding their business.

Retail businesses available as franchises include stores that sell books, clothes, flowers, frames, gifts, greeting cards, groceries, hardware, craft and hobby items, shoes, and tools. There are also convenience store franchises, discount and dollar store franchises, gas station franchises, and so on.

Buying a Franchise

The buy-in amount of franchises varies tremendously, but you need a minimum of $20,000 cash and a net worth of at least $100,000. For this, the franchisee gets many advantages. For the most part, a franchise form of business has a lower risk factor than opening a business on your own and the highest level of support. Think of it as buying into a club. The franchisor supplies club members with proven marketing techniques, training, operating systems, and extensive, ongoing support to make the business a success. This is especially desirable for those people who know they want to go into business for themselves but lack direct experience in running a business or in retail. The buyer of the franchise is never alone and gets support every step of the way; the franchisor teaches the franchisees everything they need to know.

One of the greatest advantages in purchasing a franchise is that many of the customers who frequent the store are already familiar with the product line, so they don't need to be sold on the product. The franchisor often provides national advertising that helps bring in more customers. In many instances all the customer of the franchise needs to know is where the franchise is located, and they will come.

The biggest disadvantage in purchasing a franchise is that the rules can be quite strict as to how the business is run. Sometimes the franchisor even dictates the decor of the building. These rules are in place to protect the integrity of the business. If the franchisee decides to do things differently from the way the franchisor has directed, the integrity of the product may be compromised and the customer may not get the product that he or she is accustomed to. This hurts not only the franchisee, but the franchise as well.

People who are successful franchise owners are comfortable with moderate risk and are willing to follow the rules put forth by the franchisor. They also share the same attitudes as other retail business owners, in that they have outstanding people skills and are willing to put in the hours to make the business work.

Successful franchise owners have spent countless hours researching different franchises. They have talked with current franchisees to see if they are happy with the franchisor and to find out if the franchisor lived up to expectations in terms of training and support.

Those individuals who are not good candidates to be franchise owners are those who very much want to be completely in charge of their businesses and not have anyone tell them how to run things. Or, if the individual already has extensive experience in many areas of business such as sales, accounting, and advertising, he or she may feel the services the franchise offers are not necessary.

Resources

Need more information? Below is a list of organizations and associations devoted to the retail industry, or to particular businesses within the retail industry.

Organizations and Associations

National Retail Federation (NRF)
325 7th St. NW, Suite 1100
Washington, DC 20004
Phone: 1 (800) NRF-HOW2
Fax: (202) 737-2849
www.nrf.com
The world's largest retail trade association and the publisher of *Stores* magazine.

Association for Retail Technology Standards (ARTS)
www.nrf-arts.org
An international organization dedicated to reducing the costs
of technology through standards; part of the NRF.

Association for Operations Management (APICS)
5301 Shawnee Rd., Alexandria, VA 22312-2317
Phone: (800) 444-2742 or (703) 354-8851
Fax: (703) 354-8106
www.apics.org
Helps their members, operations management professionals, to successfully compete and build a stronger global
economy.

GS1 US
Princeton Pike Corporate Center
1009 Lenox Dr., Suite 202, Lawrenceville, NJ 08648
Phone: (609) 620-0200
Fax: (609) 620-1200
www.uc-council.org
A barcode standards organization with over 200,000
members.

Retail Industry Leaders Association (RILA)
1700 N. Moore St., Suite 2250, Arlington, VA 22209
Phone: (703) 841-2300
Fax: (703) 841-1184
www.retail-leaders.org
Established in 1969 to support mass retail through research
and education.

International Association of Department Stores (IADS)
11-13 Rue Guersant, 75017 Paris, France
www.iads.org
The first association entirely devoted to department stores, bringing together stores from many countries to share retail expertise.

The Direct Marketing Association (DMA)
1120 Avenue of the Americas, New York, NY 10036-6700
Phone: (212) 768-7277
Fax: (212) 302-6714
www.the-dma.org
The leading global trade association of business and nonprofit organizations using direct marketing tools.

The Food Marketing Institute (FMI)
2345 Crystal Dr., Suite 800, Arlington, VA 22202
Phone: (202) 452-8444
Fax: (202) 429-4519
www.fmi.org
Conducts programs in research, education, industry relations, and public affairs for food retailers and wholesalers.

International Council of Shopping Centers (ICSC)
PO Box 26958, New York, NY 10087-6958
Phone: (646) 728-3800
Fax: (732) 694-1800
www.icsc.org
The global trade association of the shopping center industry, founded in 1957.

American Booksellers Association (ABA)
200 White Plains Rd., Suite 600, Tarrytown, NY 10591
Phone: (800) 637-0037
Fax: (914) 591-2720
www.bookweb.org
A national association that protects and promotes the interests of its members.

International Music Products Association (NAMM)
5790 Armada Dr., Carlsbad, CA 92008
Phone: (760) 438-8001
Fax: (760) 438-7327
www.namm.com
An association for companies in the music products industry that manufacture, buy, sell, or distribute musical instruments and products.

Jewelers of America (JA)
52 Vanderbilt Avenue, 19th Floor, New York, NY 10017
Phone: (800) 223-0673
Fax: (646) 658-0256
www.jewelers.org
The national association for the retail jeweler.

Museum Store Association (MSA)
4100 E. Mississippi Ave., Suite 800, Denver, CO 80246-3055
Phone: (303) 504-9223
Fax: (303) 504-9585

www.museumdistrict.com
Advances the success of cultural commerce and of the professionals engaged in it.

National Sporting Goods Association (NSGA)
1601 Feehanville Dr., Suite 300, Mt. Prospect, IL 60056
Phone: (847) 296-6742
Fax: (847) 391-9827
www.nsga.org
Helps its members profit in a competitive marketplace by providing information, education, and cost-saving services.

National Shoe Retailers Association (NSRA)
7150 Columbia Gateway Dr., Suite G, Columbia, MD 21046-1151
www.nsra.org
Founded in 1912 to improve the business performance of its members through continuing education, cost-saving benefits, and networking opportunities.

National Association of Chain Drug Stores (NACDS)
413 N. Lee St., PO Box 1417-D49, Alexandria, VA 22313-1480
Phone: (703) 549-3001
Fax: (703) 836-4869
www.nacds.org
Represents the largest component of pharmacy practice: the chain community pharmacy.

The North American Retail Hardware Association (NRHA)
5822 West 74ᵗʰ St., Indianapolis, IN 46278-1787
Phone: (317) 290-0338
Toll free: (800) 772-4424
Fax: (317) 328-4354
www.nrha.org
Provides information and services to retailers to help them be better and more profitable merchants.

North American Retail Dealers Association (NARDA)
4700 West Lake Ave., Glenview, IL 60025
Phone: (847) 375-4713
Fax: (866) 879-7505
www.narda.com
Supports independent retailers selling kitchen and laundry appliances, consumer home and mobile electronics, furniture, sewing machines, vacuum cleaners, and other consumer home products.

The American Specialty Toy Retailing Association (ASTRA)
116 W. Illinois St., Suite 5E, Chicago, IL 60610
Phone: (312) 222-0984
Toll free: (800) 591-0490
Fax: (312) 222-0986
www.astratoy.org
The largest association for companies in the toy and children's products arena.

Retail councils are found in each state. These councils were founded to promote environments that encourage retail growth in respective states by maintaining a strong voice in the state government.

Books

Going into Business for Yourself

Goldstein, Beth, *The Ultimate Small Business Marketing Toolkit* (McGraw-Hill, 2007).

Keup, Erwin J., *Franchise Bible* (Entrepreneur Press, 2007).

Kingaard, Jan, *Start Your Own Successful Retail Business* (Entrepreneur Press, 2007).

Miller, Julie, *Start Your Own Clothing Store* (Entrepreneur Press, 2003).

Murphy, Kevin, *The Franchise Handbook: A Complete Guide to All Aspects of Buying, Selling or Investing in a Franchise* (Atlantic, 2006).

Segel, Rick, *Retail Business Kit for Dummies* (For Dummies, 2001).

Specialty Retailing

Entrepreneur Press, *Start Your Own Arts and Crafts Business: Retail, Carts and Kiosks, Craft Shows, St. Fairs* (Entrepreneur Press, 2007).

Renn, Leslie D., & Lewis, Jerre G., *How to Start and Manage a Kiosk and Cart Business* (Lewis & Renn Associates, 2004).

Job Hunting

Bolles, Richard Nelson, *What Color Is Your Parachute? 2007: A Practical Manual for Job-Hunters and Career-Changers* (Ten Speed Press, rev ed., 2006).

Greene, Brenda, *Get the Interview Every Time: Fortune 500 Hiring Professionals' Tips for Writing Winning Resumes and Cover Letters* (Kaplan Business, 2004).

Whitcomb, Susan Britton, *Resume Magic: Trade Secrets of a Professional Resume Writer* (JIST Works, 3rd ed., 2006).

Business Philosophy/Retail, Biography and History/Customer Care

Colombo, George, *Killer Customer Care* (Entrepreneur Press, 2003).

Covey, Stephen R., *The 7 Habits of Highly Effective People* (Free Press, 1989).

Johnson, Spencer, *Who Moved My Cheese?* (Vermillion, 2002).

Kalman, Bobby, *Early Stores and Markets* (Crabtree, 1981).

Marcus, Stanley, *Minding the Store: A Memoir* (University of North Texas Press, 1997).

Spector, Robert, & McCarthy, Patrick D., *The Nordstrom Way: The Inside Story of America's #1 Customer Service Company* (Wiley, 1996).

Turner, Marcia Layton, *Kmart's Ten Deadly Sins: How Incompetence Tainted an American Icon* (Wiley, 2003).

Tzu, Sun, *The Art of War* (Shambhala, 2005).

Walton, Sam, *Sam Walton: Made in America* (Bantam, 1993).

Web Sites

Below is a list of web sites about business, the retail industry, and major retailers, and job web sites.

www.bizstats.com: Site providing useful business statistics.

www.cnnmoney.com: Good overall business site.

www.chainstoreage.com: This site bills itself as "the online service for retail executives," and contains information about supply-chain technology, finance and payment systems, real estate, electronic retailing, etc. Chain Store Age is a free web site, but you must register to access. A free e-mail newsletter is also available.

www.gershelbros.com: Gershel Bros. features both new and used store fixtures. It also offers free store planning to ensure you get what you need.

www.investopedia.com: A Forbes media company that contains business articles, a dictionary of business terms, exam preps, tutorials, etc.

www.lpinformation.com: This web site is from the National Retail Federation and contains information regarding loss prevention.

www.mediapost.com/research/index.cfm: Click on this site if you think you have an interest in marketing research or advertising. This site by the Center for Media Research is intended for planners and buyers of advertising media and contains results of marketing research reports and studies. A free subscription is available.

www.nrf.com: This is the web site of the National Retail Federation, or "The voice of retail worldwide." This outstanding web site contains information on virtually every facet of retail, including the latest technologies, job descriptions, and government relations. Books are available through this site, as is information on conferences and events.

www.plunkettresearch.com: Plunkett Research offers business intelligence, industry trends, statistics, market research, sales leads and corporate profiles.

www.retailindustryabout.com: For resources and information on retail technology and inventory control, this is the place.

www.retailindustry.about.com: The encyclopedia of retail information, this comprehensive site covers retail topics from A to Z. The site contains industry statistics, job descriptions, a retail glossary, information about the latest technology, merchandise management, etc. A free e-newsletter is also available.

www.retailingtoday.com: Retailing Today is another free web site, and is organized by sectors of retail, such as apparel and accessories, home and housewares, and hardlines, making it easier to get an idea of what is going on in these particular divisions.

www.reuters.com/business: All the latest business news, searchable by industry.

www.sba.gov: This is the site for the Small Business Administration (SBA), a government agency created in 1953 to aid in all aspects of creating, running, and even closing a small business. The web site contains how-to information such as creating a business plan, finding a market niche, finding a mentor, buying a business, and pricing products.

www.shop.org: This site is an association for online retailers and contains information on the best way to market in the changing world of cyberspace as well as in multichannel retailing.

www.slstoredisplays.com: S&L Store Fixtures is America's leading manufacturer and supplier of store fixtures and displays. If you're thinking about opening your own business, this is the place to view hundreds of different displays for all sorts of businesses.

Major Retailer Sites

Below is a sampling of web sites for just a few of the larger retailers. If you have an interest in working at a particular company, gather as much information as you can about the company to make certain it's a fit for you, your values, and ideals before applying. Visiting a company's web site is a good place to start. The sites below are not the sites where merchandise is sold, but instead contain information on company history, company philosophy, a listing of careers within the company, and information for investors.

www.careers.homedepot.com: For a thorough description of the nation's second largest retailer, Home Depot, click on this site. Besides a company history, this site also lists career opportunities at Home Depot stores, corporate headquarters, Expo, and the HD Supply divisions. Also of interest are videos titled "Realistic Job Preview," that detail what a sales associate and store HR manager do.

www.federated-fds.com: Web site for Macy's and Bloomingdale's. This site details strategic priorities, career information, community and foundation giving, and more.

www.jcpenney.net: This site describes the company's history and lists the current leaders in the company. It also describes all the careers within the company, the company's policy towards community relations, and what charities the company supports. A copy of the annual report is available.

www.limitedbrands.com: Limited Brands operates the following retailers: Victoria's Secret, Bath and Body Works, C.O. Bigelow, Henri Bendel, La Senza, The Limited, and The White Barn Candle Co. This site describes in detail the company mission, career opportunities, and social responsibility.

www.neimanmarcuscareers.com: Click on this site to find out what it's like to work for one of the most prestigious retailers in the country. This web site includes the Neiman Marcus story and a description of the executive development program. Job listings are also included and are searchable by job category and region.

www.targetcorp.com: This site details careers available, corporate values and company giving, company history, and so on.

www.walmartstores.com: Read all about the largest retailer on the planet, including the Wal-Mart story, careers within the company, suppliers, community giving, the international division, and much more.

www.wegmans.com/about: Have you ever considered a career in grocery retailing? If so, this may be the place, as Wegmans Food Markets was ranked number three on *Fortune's* Top 10 Best Companies to Work For in 2007. This private grocery chain is located primarily on the East Coast, and its web site gives all pertinent information.

www.wholefoods.com: Whole Foods, the world's leading natural and organic foods supermarket, is another outstanding place to work, and was ranked number five on *Fortune's* Top 10 Best Companies to Work For in 2007. This site discusses company philosophy, careers, history, community giving, and contains blogs, podcasts, and videos.

Job Web Sites

www.allretailjobs.com: This retail job site is free for job seekers.

www.careerbuilder.com: Job site listing jobs for most industries.

www.content.monster.com/resume/home.aspx: This site offers free advice on how to write a resume.

www.hotjobs.yahoo.com: Site listing jobs by category and region of the country.

www.ihireretail.com: Site listing retail jobs. Free to candidates searching for positions.

www.jobster.com: Job site listing jobs for most industries.

www.monster.com: Job site listing jobs for most industries; free for job seekers.

www.retailfit.com: Site listing retail positions.

Glossary

Accounts payable. An accounting term for money that a company owes for merchandise or services already purchased.

Accounts receivable. An accounting term for money that is owed to a company for merchandise already sold.

Aftermarket sales department. A department within an automotive dealership that sells service contracts and insurance to buyers.

Anchor. A large store, usually a department store, that draws customers into a mall. Anchors are almost always located at the ends of the mall or at the end of a line of stores within the mall.

B2B. Stands for *business-to-business,* and refers to the exchange of products, services, and information between businesses rather than B2C, or business-to-consumer. Forecasters are predicting that B2B revenues will soon exceed B2C revenues.

B2C. Stands for *business-to-consumer,* referring to the traditional method of retailing.

Barter. The exchange of goods without the use of money.

Black Friday. The day after Thanksgiving, which is traditionally the start of the Christmas shopping season and the most profitable day of the year for many retailers. Sales figures from Black Friday are used to project figures for the entire Christmas season. The word *black* refers to the fact that when finances were done by hand, black ink indicated a profit, while red ink indicated a loss.

Boutique retailers. Boutiques strive to serve a narrow segment of the market, satisfying the needs of a limited number of people. Boutiques often stock exclusive, one-of-a-kind merchandise, such as jewelry or designer clothing.

Brick and click. Retail companies who do some, but less than 90 percent, of their retail business online.

Career path. A solid plan detailing where people want to be in their career over the next five or ten years, or even longer. The plan includes educational, training, and experience requirements necessary to get them where they want to go.

Catalog. A pamphlet or publication listing items for sale.

Category killer. A store, almost always large, that so dominates its retail category that it winds up "killing" the competition. Small, local stores are often unable to compete with these stores.

Caveat emptor. A Latin phrase that literally means "let the buyer beware." In ancient Rome, the buyer had little recourse if a purchase did not work out.

Chain stores. Stores that have the same name, carry the same merchandise, and belong to one company.

Collectibles. Merchandise such as action figures or die-cast models, trading cards, or plush animals.

College internship. An internship is a supervised work/learning experience in which a student gains actual experience in a particular field. Internships are usually available to juniors and seniors.

Commission. Under a commission system, retail salespeople receive a percentage of the total sales they generate in addition to a salary or hourly wage. Commissions are generally paid to employees who sell big ticket items, such as furniture, cars, men's suits, or jewelry.

Consolidation. A trend in many industries, such as the automotive sales industry. Smaller dealers are giving way to larger establishments that are able to offer consumers lower prices and more services.

Construction management. The coordination of the building of a new store. Construction management is a responsibility of the store development department.

Consumer confidence. An economic term referring to the level of optimism consumers have about the economy. Consumer confidence tends to be high when inflation and unemployment rates are low. This measure is vitally important to retailers because they use it to predict future sales. When consumers feel confident, they spend more money.

Cyber Monday. The Monday after Thanksgiving, which is one of the busiest days of the year for e-retailers. Retailers speculate that people shop online on this day either because they chose not to shop at all in traditional stores during the Thanksgiving weekend or because they did not find what they wanted. Compare this with Black Friday.

Cyber security. Maintaining security for all computer systems within a company.

Cyber terrorism. The intentional attack of information systems, computer systems, and data. Cyber terrorism is fast becoming one of the biggest concerns for companies.

Demographics. Characteristics making up a group, such as age, gender, income, educational levels, and postal code. Marketers use demographic information to identify their customers. Once a demographic profile is created of the average customer, it can in turn drive advertising.

Department stores. A physically large retail store organized into many departments such as women's clothing, lingerie, linens, men's clothing, furniture, appliances, and hardware. These stores are often the anchor stores at malls or are located in the heart of downtown areas. Examples include Sears, JCPenney, Macy's, and Saks Fifth Avenue.

Direct-response advertising. A form of advertising, such as catalogs, direct mail, and television, that promotes the selling of merchandise directly to the buyer rather than through a store.

Discount department store. A department store that offers merchandise at deeply discounted prices, and usually has checkout counters located in the front of the store. Examples include Wal-Mart, Target, and Kmart.

Dry goods. Dry goods are retail products that do not require refrigeration or freezing to maintain. Dry goods are traditionally products such as clothing or fabric, or farm implements.

E-commerce. This stands for *electronic commerce* and refers to the buying and selling of goods and services on the internet; also known as e-retailing and e-tailing.

Electronic article surveillance. One of the prime methods of loss prevention; EAS involves tagging merchandise and then setting up security at all entrances and exits. Alarms sound when the merchandise has not had the tag properly removed.

Employee discount. One of the most attractive benefits of working in retail is the employee discount, which allows employees to purchase the store merchandise at a reduced price. The discount is usually expressed as a percentage.

End cap. The end of an aisle in a grocery store, large format store, or discount store. Special merchandise is usually featured on an end cap, such as clearance items, or new merchandise.

Entrepreneur. A person who opens and operates a business.

Fad. A trend, usually in fashion, that is short-lived.

Flexibility. Because work schedules can change from week to week in retail, workers must be willing to be flexible and accommodate their employers.

Floor planning. Determining where all the fixtures, display cases, merchandise, and cash registers are going to be placed in a business. Floor planning also considers paint, lighting and light fixtures, special equipment, and even the ceiling.

Focus groups. A focus group is a small group, usually 8–12 people, who are gathered together by marketing research professionals to discuss a new product, advertising, packaging, etc. The group is led by a moderator, and group members interact with one another. Focus groups are considered qualitative research, because results are not quantifiable.

Franchise. A business relationship between a company that wishes to distribute its goods and services, and a person who wishes to run his or her own business. The company is known as the *frachisor*, while the person buying these rights is called the *franchisee*.

Front-end supervisor. A manager responsible for all the cashiers and baggers for an entire shift; front-end supervisors are usually found in grocery stores, discount stores, large format stores, and other businesses where the cash registers are all located at the front of the store.

General merchandise. In a large format store, general merchandise is nonfood merchandise. General merchandise is comparable to dry goods.

Globalization. An increasing reliance on international markets for goods and services.

Impulse items. These items are generally inexpensive and usually located next to the cash register in grocery stores, discount stores, large format stores, or kiosks. Examples are candy, lighters, individually sized snack foods, and inexpensive jewelry.

Infomercial. This term is a blend of the words *information* and *commercial*. Infomercials are a way of selling products directly to the customer via television.

Information age. The age in which information became extremely easy to obtain, usually thought to be 1970.

Inventory management system. The way a business keeps track of inventory; for large corporations, this system is computerized so that buyers know when stock is low and needs to be reordered.

Job objective. The first step in creating a resume is creating a goal about the sort of job desired, a job objective. The job objective then determines what information you should list on the resume, such as relevant job experience and skills.

Kiosk. Refers to the open carts found in malls, airports, theme parks, and other high-traffic areas where people sell merchandise. Vendors may also sell newspapers, magazines, coffee or other refreshments, or even tickets from kiosks.

Lagging indicator. An economic indicator that changes after the economy has changed. Examples of lagging indicators include the unemployment rate, the prime rate, and labor costs.

Large format stores. Establishments that feature truly one-stop shopping; customers can purchase groceries and products usually found in drug stores or department stores.

Leading indicator. An economic indicator that changes before the economy changes, giving investors a preview of what is going to happen before it actually does. Leading indicators are watched quite closely by economists, who then make predictions about the economy. Examples include gross domestic product, building permits, inventory changes, and stock prices.

Licensed merchandise. Similar to collectibles, except that in order to sell this particular merchandise, the business selling the items must have an agreement with a company granting permission to sell the product. The Disney Company is a prime example of a company involved in licensed merchandise. Another example is action figures created from books and movies.

Loss leader. A loss leader is an item marked down to cost or below cost. The motive is to draw customers into the store to purchase this item, and then hopefully buy other items in the store at the same time.

Mall. A large enclosed center containing retail businesses and restaurants. Mall space tends to be more expensive to rent that strip center space. The first enclosed mall was opened in Edina, Minnesota, in 1956.

Management training program. A program, usually offered to recent college graduates, in which new hires are trained in various departments of a company to prepare them to eventually become managers.

Manufacturing. The creation of products, almost always by machine. Manufactured products are in turn sold wholesale to retailers, who mark up the price of the products, and sell them to the consumer.

Markdown. Cutting the sales price. Most retailers mark down merchandise that has been in the store for a certain period of time.

Marketing. The marketing process involves many functions, including creating the product and its features, determining how it will be distributed, deciding how the product will be promoted or advertised, and figuring out the price to charge for the product.

Marketing activity report. A report detailing the results for a particular product, line, department, or store.

Marketing plan. A detailed plan for marketing a product or line of products. Marketing plans can also be created for entire stores and companies, and may contain such details as advertising budgets.

Marketing research. A process in which information is gathered about the company's customers and their wants and needs, or the company's competition in order to improve marketing decisions. Research conducted is either primary or secondary.

Markup. The difference between the actual cost of the item to the retailer and the price the retailer sets.

Multichannels. Integrating all of the channels of distribution, such as store, web site, and catalog.

Niche marketing. Refers to a specialized yet profitable corner of the market, that is, offering a product or service that is unique in a market that needs what you are selling.

Nonstore retailer. These businesses are organized to sell goods to the public, but the place of business is not in a store. Included in this category are those who sell through the internet, infomercials, direct-response advertising, catalogs, door-to-door selling, in-home demonstrations, and vending machines.

Odd price. Choosing to price items on odd numbers, usually ending in the number nine, that is, pricing an item at $1.99 instead of $2.00.

Perpetual inventory. A sophisticated inventory management system that tracks inventory from the point it arrives to when it is purchased and then re-orders the item if necessary.

Point-of-sale registers. A point-of-sale register is basically a computer. It can handle credit and debit card transactions, record customer transactions, connect to other computers in the network, and track inventory.

Primary research. One of two means market researchers use to find information, primary research is new research designed and conducted by the company or market research firm to answer a specific question. Compare with secondary research.

Private-label merchandise. Merchandise manufactured exclusively for one retailer.

Product development. An area of marketing in which new products are created to meet the needs of the market.

Promotion. One of the 4 Ps of marketing, promotion usually refers to advertising, or how the product will be "promoted" in the marketplace.

Pure play. Retailers who close at least 90 percent of their selling transactions online.

Qualitative research. Qualitative research almost always takes the form of a focus group, in which small numbers of customers or potential customers are gathered to give their reactions to products, advertising, pricing, or distribution methods. Unlike quantitative research, there is usually no fixed set of questions, but more of a discussion. Results are not expressed numerically. The purpose of qualitative research is to get a better understanding of the customers' reactions.

Quantitative research. The goal of quantitative research is to be able to express results of research numerically, such as "62 percent of respondents are extremely happy with the product." Quantitative research almost always takes the form of the survey.

Quantity discount. Allowing a discount for purchasing in bulk. Huge retailers are able to offer lower prices to their customers than individual stores because they are able to buy such large quantities of merchandise from their vendors.

Rack jobber. A wholesaler who is allowed into a retail store to install, stock, and replenish items in a fixture.

Real estate portfolios. The land that a company owns. Plans must be created to utilize the land in the most profitable way for the company, whether it be by developing new stores or properly maintaining existing properties. This responsibility falls under the domain of the store development manager.

Retail. Selling goods directly to consumers.

Retail Sales Indicator. A monthly report issued by the United States Census Bureau that measures the goods sold in the retail industry. This index is considered to be a leading indicator of the economy, and gives officials an indication of consumer confidence.

Rounder. A round fixture.

Seasonality. Refers to the fact that many retail businesses have variations in their sales due to the season of the year. For many retailers, the Christmas season is the busiest.

Secondary research. One of the two ways marketing research professionals gather information is by using information that is already out there, such as government figures or syndicated studies.

Shrinkage. The loss of merchandise in a store. Shrinkage may result from shoplifting, employee theft, inaccurate paperwork, or simply misplacement. Shrinkage eats up profits and drives up prices for goods.

Small Business Administration (SBA). The government agency whose mission is to promote and aid small businesses. The SBA offers three different loan programs.

Specialty expertise. A salesperson who is an expert in a line of merchandise, for example, a salesperson selling jewelry may choose to specialize, becoming a gemologist. Specialty expertise often leads to the salesperson making more money.

Specialty retailing. In the retail industry, specialty retailing refers to selling from kiosks.

Start-ups. Opening a new store for a company or even an entirely new business. Working in a start-up can be stressful, but those who have experience getting start-ups up and running profitably are immensely valuable to the company.

Stock clerk. A person who restocks the shelves with merchandise. Stock clerks work in grocery stores and other large retail businesses.

Store maintenance management. The responsibility of the store development manager, store maintenance means ensuring that existing stores are kept up to company standards and planning remodeling for those store locations that require it.

Store retailer. A fixed location designed to attract a high volume of walk-in traffic. This is the way most of us still buy things, through store retailers.

Strategy of alternating. Refers to working in different departments in a large corporation so as to gain a better understanding of how the entire company works. Alternating often prepares individuals to reach the upper levels of a company. For example, individuals often work as buyers at company headquarters, then move into a store position, then alternate back to a higher buying position at corporate headquarters.

Strip center. A "strip" of land in which several retailers are located. Customers generally park right in front of the store or in a lot and walk directly into the store, as opposed to a mall, which is enclosed. Strip centers also differ from malls in that they usually do not have anchor stores.

Suppliers. The vendors, usually manufacturers, who supply merchandise to retailers.

Supply chain. A network of all the businesses involved in getting merchandise to the consumer; this network includes material suppliers, manufacturers, transportation companies, storage facilities, and retailers. Disruptions in any one of the operations of these businesses such as labor strikes, or raw material shortages may result in the disruption of the flow of products to the consumer.

Turnarounds. Refers to a business that is not run well or is not profitable, and needs to be turned around. Sometimes a turnaround can even be one particular store in a chain of stores that is otherwise profitable. Turning around a business can be stressful, but those individuals who can do this successfully are invaluable in the marketplace.

Turnkey operation. This is an option in kiosk marketing where the owner pays extra for the entire operation to be set up, almost like a franchise. All the owner has to do to start the business is to "turn the key."

Values. A person's principles or morals.

Visual merchandising. The art of creating displays or arranging merchandise in the most appealing fashion, thereby creating more sales.

Warehouse club stores. One of the fastest growing segments, these stores feature low prices as the main attraction. Items are often sold in bulk, customers are usually required to pay a yearly fee to join, and little is offered in the way of customer service.

White space. Refers to the open area on a page, the portion not covered in words. Good resumes have white space on the page to be visually appealing. **Wholesale.** The price a manufacturer charges the retailer for a product. The retailer then marks up the price to the consumer.

Wholesaler. A company, usually a manufacturer, that provides goods to the retailer, that in turn sells them to the consumer.

Word-of-mouth. Refers to one of the most effective forms of advertising, when one consumer recommends a product or business to another.

Index